Create and Prosper
Claiming Your Power and Worth

Antoinette Spurrier

Create and Prosper

Copyright © 2012 by Antoinette Spurrier

All rights reserved. No part of this book may be reproduced or transmitted in any form or by any means without written permission of the author.

First published by Lightning Source June 2012, Second edition 2015

ISBN: 978-0-9903824-9-2 (hardcover)
        978-0-9903824-8-5 (paperback)

Library of Congress Control Number: TK

Printed in the United States of America

*This book is dedicated to my mother, Yvonne,
who has been my lifelong best friend, and to
John McLaurin who personified eternal friendship.*

Contents

Introduction 1

I Cultivating Creativity 7

II Aligning Your Dual Natures: Limited Self and Eternal Self................................. 49

III Deservedness and How to Feel It............... 77

IV Abundance and Prosperity..................... 107

GOLD VASE FLORAL

By Yvonne G. Christenson

Introduction

To the Reader,

Create and Prosper: Claiming Your Power and Worth is the second edition of a book previously titled *Creativity and Abundance: Claiming Your Power and Worth*. It is also one installment in my six-book series that began with *Deliberate Happiness: The Complete Guide*. This shorter work distills themes from several related chapters in the larger book into practical exercises to ignite your creativity, align your dual natures, confront and remove deservedness issues and thus lead you toward a life of abundance and prosperity.

My desire is to inspire powerful transformation by tapping into your own consciousness and creativity. Then, through a process of introspection and practice, you may bring about fundamental changes in your sense of deservedness and thus allow yourself to manifest abundance and prosperity in your life and work. When properly applied, spiritual principles and techniques, including affirmations and meditation, can lead to greater personal and spiritual empowerment. I thus invite you to become a co-creator with the Divine in reflection and action. Now is the time to claim your creativity and abundance.

Deliberate Happiness: The Complete Guide offers a detailed analysis of the background to these practices and an explanation of the natural patterns and scientific laws governing psychological and spiritual growth. In this smaller volume, I focus on techniques and ideas that, with patience and persistence, will stoke the fires of your creativity and help remove any deservedness issues that thwart your full expression and manifestation of abundance. These techniques include:

- Spiritual practices, such as meditation, visualizations, journaling, introspection and especially affirmations, energized by the application of will.
- A definition of success, health and wealth that focuses beyond the material to a deeper awareness of your Divine nature.
- Techniques to uproot negative self-talk and alter long-standing feelings of worthlessness that sabotage creativity, love, happiness and manifesting abundance.
- A realistic focus on the power of affirmations to help overcome negative thoughts and behaviors that confront us when we seek to express our creative natures.

My intention is to issue this sacred invitation to claim the most of yourself through self-understanding and proven techniques in personal transformation. As you better understand spiritual law and these techniques, you will become a Co-Creator with the source of all creation.

I discovered these spiritual techniques and practices through first-hand experience. Trained in the field of psychology with an emphasis in family counseling and a specialty in treating chemical dependency, my professional life was dramatically interrupted by the onset of a life-threatening, catastrophic illness that challenged me to confront a total upheaval of my beliefs, health and previous capacities.

After surviving continuing medical challenges, I entered into a period of profound personal change that awakened me to a spiritual layer of reality and led on to the evolution of a new and much larger spiritual perspective. I developed an interest in meditation, affirmations and visualization as healing modalities and as tools of growth

Introduction

and empowerment. Each of this book's major chapters ends with suggested affirmations relating to the chapter's theme.

As a spiritual counselor, I have shared these discoveries and approaches with many others, and have seen their profound impact upon those who practice them with sincere belief, patience, persistence and dedication.

Creativity is your birthright; when you remove obstacles to viewing yourself as a Co-Creator with the Divine, you will better be able to express your own uniqueness and manifest abundance and prosperity, eventually returning to your natural state of happiness and joy. You have the inherent power and worth to create more deliberate happiness.

Congratulations on taking this first step!

Antoinette Spurrier

San Diego, California
Spring, 2016

GREEN FORREST

By Yvonne G. Christenson

CHAPTER I

CULTIVATING CREATIVITY

You are invited to awaken your true nature and to express yourself fully in every way, every day as a dynamic co-creator with the Divine.

KEY TOPICS ADDRESSED IN THIS CHAPTER:

- Creativity is not a specific talent, finite and limited in origin. Like all of us, you possess the spark of creativity within.
- Creativity is part of your spiritual nature, not an attribute of personality. With greater awareness of your spiritual nature, you will activate the creative force itself.
- Creativity may be further accessed by a more harmonious alignment between the Limited Self and the Eternal Self.
- Creativity may be harnessed by using meditation, visualization, and affirmations, among other techniques. Affirmations can dramatically increase your efforts to expand your awareness of the creative force and your Eternal Self.

Creativity is Infinite

You are invited to tap the well of creativity within, the dynamic, ever-present force that will allow you to co-create with the Divine and in that partnership and that flow, experience true happiness. Creativity is not an attribute of personality, nor is it limited to a certain type of artistic person. Creativity is intrinsically tied to your spiritual nature and ultimately to your feelings of happiness. You do not "acquire" it. You simply need to activate that which is already present within. The spark of creativity that ignites the stars, forms universes, and gives color to the flowers, is within you, and all of us as well. It makes us feel alive, connected to our human family, to nature, beauty and the cosmos. Creativity provides the deepest sense of joy and well-being.

At times in your life creative effort may seem out of reach. You may cast a longing gaze at the artists of the world thinking you are missing the creative "gene" that was their endowment. Why do some people seem to have greater creative ability than others? If you have it, why haven't you manifested it in your life?

Whether you experience its presence or not, the seed of creativity *is* within. It is part of the cosmic energy of the universe itself, and thus the very origin of your divine nature. You have the power to tap into and access the expansive flow of creation at any time. Expanding your creative aspect within is a spiritual opportunity and a divine promise.

You were born out of the vision of God. The Creator of All instilled within you the power of creativity itself as your spiritual birthright. Your conditions and circumstances are precisely perfect to call you to this self-awakening, for the divinity within desires to co-create with you. Still, messages from your family, your culture, even your own experiences may have led you to mistaken ideas about your creative capacity.

Examples of false ideas about creativity:

- I am not a creative person.
- My creativity is limited.
- I don't have any special creative talents.
- I am not an artist, writer, musician, etc.
- It's too late for me to become creative.
- People are either born creative or they're not.
- I can't be creative and also make money.
- I don't know how to access, or unlock, my creativity.
- I need to be sensible and forget creative fulfillment in my life.
- Creativity is impractical and not marketable.
- My creativity is not worthwhile to pursue.
- Creativity is limited and finite, therefore accessible only to a few.
- Creativity cannot express through me, for I am an inferior channel.

Any of these negative ideas can become circular, denying the powerful truth of your innate creativity and your status as a channel of inspiration, beauty, and artistry. You must unlock your creativity by changing your thoughts and self-definition.

What is Creativity?

Creativity is our true nature; blocks are an unnatural thwarting of a process at once as normal and as miraculous as the blossoming of a flower at the end of a slender green stem.

JULIA CAMERON, *The Artist's Way*

Creativity is often viewed from too narrow a perspective. We may think of it as simply an attribute of personality, or link it only to specific talents or abilities: "Others are creative; I am not." When we view creativity only as expressed through specific talents, we further minimize it by claiming that those talents are impractical.

> *Imagination is the beginning of creation. You imagine what you desire, you will what you imagine and at last you create what you will.*
>
> GEORGE BERNARD SHAW

Creativity can never have narrow constraints or definitions because it is a part of All that Is. It is woven into the very atoms. Every aspect of life springs forth out of the fullness of creative energy. As you expand your definition of yourself as a profound part of creation, you will open to infinite possibilities. You will begin to see yourself as a creative being with unique and potent ways of expressing life, personality, talents, insights, and intuition. As you harness your imagination and ride it into the heavenly realm, you will no longer see yourself as a mere finite expression of a physical being limited by the body.

In truth, your finite form came from the act of creation. The infinite part of you has never been limited. This understanding frees you to be a co-creator with Life itself. In her book, "The Zen of Creative Painting," author Jeanne Carbonetti writes, "Creativity is a mystery. That's the great secret to unearthing its treasures. For what you seek to explore and to fathom is really yourself. From the moment you are born, your birthright is to play with the great creative process that is your life."

CREATIVITY UNLEASHES YOUR INHERENT POWER

Creativity is the breath of the gods, giving life, joy, and inspiration to your human existence. It bridges heaven and earth. When you are in tune with your creative nature, you step into a dimension that allows you to explore the heights and depths of your spiritual nature.

The words and attitudes of others, as well as the successes and disappointments of others, have impacted your sense of creativity. If you see yourself as lacking creative talents or the character of an artist, can you identify the origin of such self-assessments? Can you remember specific messages about creative insufficiencies? Was creativity encouraged or discouraged when you were a child?

Regardless of the messages you received as a child, it is never too late to tap into this dynamo within. The brilliant painter, Henry Matisse, succinctly put it this way: "Creativity takes courage." It takes courage to overcome self-doubt, to try new things, to face our vulnerabilities and to embark on new adventures. Creative effort begins with intention. All journeys begin with a focused aim, followed by will-directed activity.

TOOLS THAT ENHANCE CREATIVITY

Several principles and practices, listed below, are the means by which you can open to your creativity, as well as your own self-empowerment. Exploring your consciousness and examining your habitual patterns of thought will help you to access your natural creative abilities.

- **Imagination** – Examine the role imagination and intuition play in your life at present.

- **Self permission** for growth – Open yourself to change and releasing fear.
- **Dynamic intention** – Trust the power within to create what you intend.
- **Dynamic willpower** – Believe that focused intention, fueled by spirit, energizes the power of will.
- **Visualization** – See yourself as a creative being doing creative acts and arriving at creative solutions.
- **Affirmations** – Assert your potency as creator of your destiny.
- **Meditation** – Emphasize your interiorized consciousness.

We all approach our creativity in different ways. For some, walking through nature inspires their inner muse; for others, meditation or listening to music. Your creativity may speak to you in silence or when you visit places of artistic beauty, such as the Louvre. The well known poet, David Whyte, spoke of accessing creativity through a deep inner conversation with the self: "You've got to find that contact point as an individual. Ask the question, 'Where am I interested? Where, in a very short time, do I become passionate once I've opened up that initial interest? What do I have energy for? And will I have faith enough to actually spend enough time so that I can open up that door into what, to begin with, is a new territory, but eventually becomes my new home?' "

Mahatma Gandhi also reminds us that we have the answers within: **"Everyone who wills can hear the inner Voice. It is within everyone."**

Tuning in to this inner voice and hearing its message will bring forth the deeper clarity you are seeking. Remember that creative expression has no limitation. It is what moves you uniquely. What you feel, and how you are moved, will be unlike anyone else's feelings and inspirations. All new inventions began with the spark of unique creativity – bringing something into the world that no one had dreamed of before.

Introspection Exercise: Diving Deep

- List five experiences during which you felt, or demonstrated, some form of creativity, even if you were a child at the time. This may include areas of expression such as writing a poem or song, creating a drawing, or having a creative idea.
- List comments that you remember about how someone else saw your creative talents.
- Did you hear discouraging or encouraging statements about your creative interests or attempts? Which statements were predominant?
- Did you internalize any of these ideas, thoughts, or experiences? If so, which ones?
- Did any inspire or restrict your passionate interest in any area of specific creative endeavor? If so, how?

Definitive statements and assessments about your creative expression have a potent effect, for better or worse. Professor of Art Education and author David London wrote, "All statements marking good and bad, like and dislike, in some fashion damage our spirit and consequently lead us to pull on our defensive armor. This is a terribly steep price to pay for what is actually desired in the exchange: increased capacity for breadth of imagination and clarity of expression." If we lacked encouragement, especially in our formative years, there is a good chance our creativity was stunted.

> *Creative success, above all, can be defined as that which is joy-producing to your true nature.*

Whatever detrimental effects there may be from your past, however stymied you may feel in your creative endeavors, you *can change*. To desire more creativity is a start. If you reflect on returning to an area of creative interest, that is movement. As we back that reflection with focused intention, it will eventually come to pass. Creativity is your birthright and is always there for you, however obscured it may be.

Make a Dream List

Make a dream list of those creative areas that you would like to expand. Prioritize the top two areas. Do not hesitate to list interests in which you have had no previous experience. If you have always wanted to play a musical instrument, put it down on the list even if you feel intimidated by the prospect. Give yourself permission to try a new area. How will you build confidence by refusing to begin and to try? Here are some suggestions for creating your dream list:

a) **Unleash your imagination**: Give yourself permission to name your dreams, identify your hopes, desires and what you believe will make you happy. Remember, creativity has no limits.

b) **Identify areas of creative interest**. What interested you as a child? Were you drawn to color, or fantasy, dance or mechanics? Be sure not to censor any area because you believe it's impractical.

c) **Creativity is an experiment in expanding awareness**: Select a couple of areas in which you desire to begin creative exploration.

d) **As you see yourself, so you become**: Imagine yourself successfully, joyously working in the areas of interest you just identified. As you imagine, you cast a blueprint of the future which has the power to become manifest.

e) **Set aside time**: Structure some time to begin exploring and working with these interests.

f) **Dynamic intention:** With focused intention, visualize and affirm your creativity.

g) **Integrate creativity into daily life:** Let creativity enliven your work, family, romantic and spiritual life. Every aspect can benefit from the creative flair within.

Giving Yourself Permission to Change

Have you ever wondered what gets in the way of claiming your own happiness? If happiness is so important, why isn't it easier to attain? One reason is that the Limited Self becomes attached to its own limitation. Human nature tends to hold on to what is familiar, even if it is confining or brings discontent. Before any change can happen, you must give yourself permission to release those parts that resist change. You must embrace your worthiness to succeed. Resistance to new endeavors clips the wings upon which your creativity can soar heaven-bound.

By giving yourself permission to change, imagination will stir and gain momentum to move along new lines. The commitment to change and open to your creativity must precede any effective thrust of will.

Will is the energetic spark that ignites all worthy endeavors. To desire without energy, to desire without vision, is to invite stagnation and reduce the possibilities of full claiming. You must first place your intention upon your creative desires. Intention will begin to stir dynamic will-based energy. Intention is your broadcast to the Divine and to the divinity within and will summon response from the universal divine energy that is ever supporting your endeavors. Your unfolding and expansion is of vital interest to the Source of all.

Becoming Fearless

Perhaps you harbor fears about undertaking new creative efforts. If so, you might ask yourself, "What is the worst thing that can happen to me if I try and do not succeed?" You are redefining yourself as a risk-taker by taking action in spite of the fear. Learning to take risks will expand access to your creativity. And it will begin to shrivel up the power of fear.

Once you have given yourself permission to change and to redefine yourself as a creative being, you will need to keep reminding yourself of your commitment. As you embrace positive change wholeheartedly, you begin a process that opens you to the Universal Flow. You find yourself supported by powerful forces of the Universe. You ignite the creative force within, and blaze with new possibilities. Your true artistry is born.

Regardless of your particular habit patterns, feelings of unworthiness, lack of self-confidence or negative self-talk, if you continue to make the effort, you will be victorious. Be patient! If the pace of your progress disappoints you, keep moving toward change anyway.

History is filled with inspiring examples of artists who persevered despite great odds. In 1913 when Igor Stravinsky debuted his now famous *The Rite of Spring*, audiences rioted. Yet it was this very work that changed the way composers in the 20th century thought about music; the work cemented his place in modern musical history. Today Monet's paintings sell for millions of dollars and hang in some of the most prestigious institutions in the world. Yet during his own time, his work was mocked and rejected by the artistic elite, the Paris Salon. Monet kept at his impressionist style, which caught on and became a springboard for major changes to art that ushered in the modern era.

Had either Stravinsky or Monet lacked patience and perseverance, or succumbed to negative or self-defeating thoughts, the world would never have been graced with their unique artistic expression.

Their examples, and many others, should encourage you in your efforts to free yourself from self-doubt. Much like the onion that is formed in layers, your layers of false

> *Once you make a decision, the universe conspires to make it happen.*
> RALPH WALDO EMERSON

thoughts must be peeled away, one by one, in order for you to shed them. Acts of change and empowerment begin with permission to change, redefine yourself, and imagine.

CREATIVITY AND IMAGINATION

Creativity and imagination are synergistic. Imagination inspires creativity and forms the seed thoughts that are then cultivated into myriad outer expressions. *Creativity begets more creativity.* The more you unleash its latent power, the more you have. The more you have, the more unbounded is its expression in you.

To imagine is to cast an image into a light form by using your mind. The more you exercise imagination, the greater the potential for creating seed thoughts and direct creative expressions. To imagine means that you are a painter in the light, and a sculptor and form maker in the light. Nothing will materialize without the light image being cast first. The source of that imagination is Spirit—a vast sea of limitless Spirit. As you use your mental abilities in this way, you are remaking your life, accessing creative power, and unlocking the potency and the potential of who you truly are.

CREATIVITY AND LOVE

An energized heart is a creative heart. An energized heart is expansive in loving. By contrast, stagnation of energy in the heart center diminishes the creative flow. If you would expand your creativity, you must increase your loving.

To live in the love vibration is to activate the heart center. The heart expands by the act of giving. It is out of love and union that

> *Creativity is our true nature; blocks are an unnatural thwarting of a process at once as normal and as miraculous as the blossoming of a flower at the end of a slender green stem.*
>
> JULIA CAMERON,
> *The Artist's Way*

creativity expresses itself in the highest way with the conception of a child. From seed energy, the embryo is formed, and from the embryo, the baby is born. When love is in the heart of the mother and father, that very vibration enters into the seed (the ovum/sperm). Through love, creation occurs. Through continuous loving, creation is enhanced.

To encourage greater creativity in life, love more, give more, and serve more, selflessly. This loving, giving, and serving will further create an alignment between your Limited and Eternal Selves. The greater the alignment, the more you will experience congruency with your deeper nature and with the flow of life itself. This is the key to manifesting your dreams. All of these elements are involved in energizing the heart. Loving is the key to this expansion.

One method of activating the heart center is to concentrate on the spine and consciously bring energy from the lower section of the spinal column near the tailbone, up toward the dorsal area of the spine opposite the heart. Once the energy has been centered in the heart center, broadcast the energized feeling outward in expanding waves of love. This technique is widely used by adherents of Yoga and many other spiritual paths to develop love and compassion.

CREATIVITY: THE LIMITED SELF AND THE ETERNAL SELF

If you believe creativity is primarily an expression of the Limited Self, then creativity, by its nature, is limited. This narrow vantage point ties you to your physical, psychological identity in the material world. From the perspective of the Limited Self, not only is supply limited, but manifestation has finite restriction. Belief in finite restriction significantly stunts the expression of creativity.

For the Limited Self, creativity combines skill sets, specific abilities, and/or attributes. If you measure your personal worthiness in this way, you will perceive limitations in your capacity to express creativity. Your creativity then becomes limited, tied to faulty self-definitions and issues of deservedness.

Creativity and the Eternal Self

Creativity, as viewed from the vantage point of the Eternal Self, is another thing entirely. You not only possess, but also *are* a powerhouse that can tap the dynamic force of creation itself. The nature of the Eternal Self is beyond any limit whatsoever. You will learn much more about the nature of your two selves—Limited and Eternal—and how to align and integrate them in Chapter Two, but for now let's take an introductory look at how your dual nature relates to your creativity.

If we consider the possibilities of creativity from the perspective of the Eternal Self, which knows its lineage is with the Creator of all, then we know it is incapable of experiencing the idea of separation from the Creator. The inward diving into those still waters of Spirit will harvest the pearls of that Self in all their luminous glory. In the silence, creativity flows. In the imagination, creativity flourishes. In will-directed activity, creativity manifests.

As you increase your alignment within yourself, the Limited and Eternal Selves enter into harmony and thus, greater authenticity. There is no "pretend" or presumption. The ego-based personality falls away, giving birth to a more refined, integrated being. You sense a new centeredness within your core nature—the soul—which naturally aligns with the limitless universe and the power and force of creation itself.

The Passion of Suffering versus the Passion of Joy

Whatever the form of artistic expression, whether it is painting, music, writing, poetry, dance, etc., there are those who believe that suffering is necessary. This popular misconception—that artistic expression requires nearly unbearable sacrifice and suffering—has been fueled by images of tormented artists throughout history and in contemporary culture. True artistic passion can exist in suffering. But passion can exist as well in divine expression and joy.

While some have managed to create great art from their suffering, deep and great agony rarely translates into enduring artistic endeavors. Suffering and joy are not static, but move as energy lines in creation. They also generate either a negative flow of energy or a positive flow of energy in the universal flow. How you experience passion, with either suffering or joy, creates in you a legacy of consciousness habits. If you are interested in having your artistic expression emanate from joy, then you should consider developing a greater alignment with the Eternal Self.

For some, of course, art flows out of a deep sense of joy, love, abundance and the desire to express and share their creative gifts. For others, the idea that a joy-filled consciousness can create deeply felt art may be challenging. However, passion is present in both creation and in destruction. Passion exists in polarity. Where and how you channel that passion, will determine, to some degree, how you move those lines of energy. Remember that these moving lines of energy also have the power of magnetism and attraction. The movement of energy continues to operate by the law of attraction, whether it is criticized, rejected, exalted or embraced. How you participate in your passion brings forth new lines of magnetic attraction.

A kind of happiness may be based upon self-indulgence of the Limited Self. Joy, on the other hand, is the domain of the Eternal Self. Except with a Christ-like figure of true spiritual stature, suffering cannot uplift the consciousness of others or yourself. Suffering, without enlightenment, can simply be an invitation for others to join in shared misery.

The passion of joy also can also emanate from and continue resonating from within the universe itself. The passion of suffering, on the other hand, continues to emanate, but that emanation ties you to a negative flow of energy. With an effort to access more of your joy-filled nature, you can tap into and experience creativity to the fullest. Whether you desire to express the passion associated with suffering or the passion associated with joyous expansion is up to you.

If you desire greater self-integration, you will discover that the universe is on tap for your wildest dreams. Creativity is not limited to your earthly experiences, but also contains the primordial energy of all experience, all passion, and all joy. The Source of creativity within you is brimming with possibilities and always ready to support, encourage and inspire you. Aligned with it, your discoveries are transcendent and illuminating, for you were born to be a creator.

CREATIVITY: WE UNLEASH IT. WE DON'T ACQUIRE IT

Your real power is not in the acquisition of creativity, but in the unlocking and unleashing of the dormant power of the Creator within. This occurs when you open to your divine nature. You express more creativity when you:

- Claim creativity as your birthright.
- Explore your dreams and inspirations.
- Make time for creative endeavors.
- Journal as a creative tool. (A good resource is *The Artists' Way* by Julia Cameron.)

- Become more aware/conscious of what holds you back and work on reversing those thoughts/behaviors.
- Visualize and affirm creativity.

Exploring your Dreams as Sources of Inspiration and Creativity

No dream can manifest without first allowing yourself to dream. What are your most precious dreams? What are the hopes and desires you want to experience? The dreams you dream in your waking state are the hopes and desires that you long to achieve. Explore these ideas, desires and urges.

Perhaps there are new areas of creative expression that you are curious about. No image can take form without the imagination. No energy can be moved forward by sheer willpower alone. You must first have the framework for it. See yourself as a powerful creator capable of recasting old roles and manufacturing new mental movie scripts in which you are more joyous, happy, and creatively expressive.

To do this, invite imagination to a new level. Envision that you are an actor creating the script of your life on the big screen. Mentally cast yourself in a creative role. What does that part look like? Does it involve a high level of performance with a specific skill? Or do you see the actor exhibiting definite attributes? Is there a specific talent, or area of mastery, you long desired to explore, exhibit, or perform? Let your imagination open fully, without entertaining any limitation. What would your life look like if you were absolutely assured of success?

To increase your capacity to imagine, practice visualizing the various roles. Combining the visualization with the successful emotional feeling state will intensify the experience. Giving form to dreams, making them concrete in your imagination, and feeling the experience *as if it were real*, will further stimulate the creative process. The time to begin is now. We must not only give ourselves permission to dream, but cast ourselves as the star performer in our personalized dream-script.

Write down your thoughts and feelings in a journal for exploring your dreams. You will only be able to explore which dreams are worth pursuing when you are fully clear about what they are.

To Dream Your Dreams, Avoid Mind-Altering Chemicals

Many habitual users of mind-altering substances believe that their hopes, desires, and dreams are more powerful and more imaginative because of the use of chemicals, drugs, or marijuana.

However, chemicals that may stimulate the flow of ideas can also paralyze the power of will to move those ideas forward. Such substances hamper the development of self-discipline. They impair the focus and direction of the energy needed to activate will power.

Creativity requires the combination of inspiration and imagination with will-based activity. At some point, thoughts and ideas must be propelled forward by concentration and dynamic will. No matter how beautiful the automobile, it will not go far without a fully functioning engine. Marijuana, among other substances, kills initiative, drive, and action. It dulls ambition and seduces the user into simply dreaming his or her dreams with no follow-through.

There are no short cuts in the effort to materialize a creative life. Imagination does not originate in chemicals, but rather stirs in the sea of Spirit and creation. Your focused intention allows you to ride the waves of inspiration and imagination in that limitless sea. Chemicals may promise oceanic experiences, but actually bind and tie users to the shores of stagnation. Regular use of marijuana and other mind-altering substances may provide the illusion of creating experiences, but in reality may prevent the actualization of them in everyday life.

An interiorized consciousness (achieved through quality meditation techniques) expands consciousness. Sedating consciousness does not interiorize it. Sedation can also create dependence upon the substance, if not chemically, then psychologically. Meditation, with quality techniques, is a superior pathway to knowing and experiencing the creative.

Dreams During the Sleep State Enhance Creativity

The pre-sleep state and actual dream experiences are powerful tools to enhance your creativity.

- Your dream life is positive proof of the power of your imagination and the gift of your inherent creativity. Your "storytelling" and image-making while asleep exhibit unbounded creativity. This should encourage you in re-defining yourself as imaginative, inspired, and creative.

- Your dream life may also function as a spiritual compass. The Eternal Self may use the language and symbols of dreams to inspire you toward greater self-knowledge and integration. The Eternal Self encourages the consciousness toward greater joy, self-knowing, and love.

- Your dreams provide a mirror of your habits of consciousness and your deepest attitudes.

Pre-sleep suggestions can allow the cycle of dreaming and sleep to improve your ability to engage in those positive behaviors when awake. Pre-sleep suggestions can incubate creative ideas and encourage your receptivity to information beyond the domain of the Limited Self. When you visualize and affirm positive suggestions as you fall asleep, you deepen your access to the universal unconscious, the God-stream of knowing. The border between waking and sleep is a powerful state. This affirmation can help tap its potential: "I give thanks, for in the sleeping state, clarity comes to me about my higher purpose, and the greatest positive use of my energy."

Many of us have never fully explored our life's higher purpose. Jobs allow us to earn income to meet obligations, but they are often not congruent with our true purpose. A higher life purpose must align with the soul's nature and the best use of time, energy, resources, and possibilities.

Are your current roles carved out by default? Have you, perhaps, been attempting to live someone else's dream? Although you have an obligation to your present circumstances, this does not mean you cannot explore other meaningful, creative aspects of life and work. If you desire greater peace, joy, and happiness, you must allow yourself to explore, imagine, and create. Such exploration does not exempt you from responsibility and attention to those dependent upon you. Yet despite such roles, you are not limited in your capacity to explore your creativity.

Your preconceptions about your identity are powerfully guarded and influenced by the ego. It readily goes into either assaultive or defensive modes of resistance, when new ideas challenge preconceptions. As you enter the pre-sleep state, the ego-based consciousness becomes less vigilant.

On the other hand, the Eternal Self has no need to defend its expansiveness in truth and in the vibration of love. The Eternal Self is simply in a state of perfect Being. Pre-sleep suggestions that resonate with the truth of the soul will guide you to response and action.

Any suggestion in the pre-sleep state will act as a stimulus for experiencing the Eternal Self. An affirmation which states, "When I sleep, I create" gives permission and direction to the subconscious to bring into your experience your most desired goals and needs. The greater the alignment and attunement between the Limited Self and the Eternal Self, the greater will be the possibility of changing impermanent states of happiness to enduring states of joy.

The technique of auto-suggestion involves these simple steps:

- Envision white light around you and give thanks that you are divinely protected and divinely inspired by the power and the force of the universe, or God. Petition a power higher than yourself in whatever manner makes you comfortable.

- After you have mentally surrounded yourself with white light, state that ideas of inspiration and creativity are now manifesting. Possible affirmations that could be used are:

My mind incubates the creative flow.
My mind is inspired with creative solutions.
I am inspired by powerful, creative solutions in
my career life and in my personal life.
Spirit inspires solutions that come to me with clarity
while in the dreaming and sleeping state.
I am creative mind. I am inventive mind. I access knowing.
I penetrate truth. I am inspired by the Infinite Thought.

In this pre-sleep state, continue to repeat any of these sentences, or other similar ideas, while focusing your energy on the screen of your forehead, at the point between the eyebrows ("spiritual eye"). Proceed with intention and receptivity, as if it is inevitable that you will receive a divine positive response. Your consciousness should not entertain doubts about your capacity to receive or create.

Keep a notebook, or paper and pencil, near your bedside to assist you in recording thoughts, ideas, or inspirations that may come to you in that resting or sleeping state. Develop the habit of writing down these thoughts; this will encourage your focus of intention and your ability to receive inspiration. Thoughts not written down or recorded may rapidly disappear. If you continue with this practice night after night, you will find that sleep incubates creative thought.

You can also do affirmations around specific creative areas, such as music, writing, and art. After you have mentally placed the white light of protection around yourself, then mentally repeat, "I am inspired in my music, art, writing, etc. The power of inspiration and creativity are manifesting in magnificent form now." Another affirmation:

As I sleep, I create.
As I sleep, I invent.
As I sleep, I solve all problems.

Time Management

The subject of time management may appear to be directly opposite the concept of creative flow. Many feel that creative flow moves with the greatest force if unhampered or unrestricted by humanity's artificial constraints. But even the most powerful river is contained on either side as it moves toward the ocean. "Containing" (managing) your time is essential if your creative flow is to move toward its fullest, most oceanic expression. Providing the proper time and place for your creativity is necessary, just as it is for any worthy endeavor.

A tempting way of avoiding your fears regarding creativity is to hide your potential behind the excuse of having no time. You must build in some structured time to exercise your creativity if it is to expand.

In reality, the more you are centered and aligned with yourself, the greater your access to inspiration, and the more connected you

> *If the consciousness can think and dream itself into bad habits, it has only to think and dream differently to form good habits. Good or bad ideas are different forms or different dreams of consciousness. It is better to dream beautiful phases of consciousness than to have nightmares. Consciousness is imaginative, sensitive, and pliable; it can think and dream itself into any state.*
>
> PARAMAHANSA YOGANANDA
> *God Talks with Arjuna, pg. 34*

are to the stream of all creation. The more fragmented you are, the less consistent is your access to that stream. You can train your pliable consciousness to become more imaginative by exercising your imagination.

The habit that we are attempting to cultivate, above all, is the habit of discipline. Discipline is directly tied to will-based intentions. Discipline strengthens will. Through discipline you can train the consciousness to increasingly imagine and visualize. When you set aside time just to imagine success in creative endeavors and to practice the habit of gratitude, you will reinforce the spiritual quality of gratitude and the habit of creativity by aligning more fully with the Creator.

You have probably experienced the desire to try something new—to paint, or to take up a musical instrument or write your memoir. Perhaps procrastination set in, and before you knew it, another year, or two, went by. There is no time like the present to begin. This requires discipline. Discipline helps us to persevere. Thomas Edison is supposed to have said, "All great ideas are 10% inspiration and 90% perspiration." Time management is critical to the cultivation of discipline and, hence, to expressing your creativity.

Discipline is also especially important in a spiritual practice, such as meditation, an essential component to a happy, creative life. Meditation is more than just a way of relaxing and entering into a heightened state of peace. Peace does not just happen by chance, nor does creativity simply appear. Rather, it is the outcome of disciplined practice. The more you meditate with keen attention, the more consistently you are able to access deeper states of consciousness. And the deeper you go into consciousness, the more your creative channel opens. Adding meditation to your daily routine can dramatically speed the progress of your creative journey.

How to be Manage Your Time More Effectively

a) Analyze how you use your time. Write down how your time is spent each day, analyzing patterns.

- Work activities.
- Recreational activities.
- Non-work activities: reading, the Internet, TV.

b) Include creative activities each day. View this "appointment" with yourself as a gift—of play and reconnection with your spirit and essence.

- Set small goals at first. Giving yourself short periods of time to work on specific projects can be a way of increasing skill and refining the use of time. Even 15-30 minutes a day will develop the habit of creativity.
- Set quality time. Spend at least 15-30 minutes a day seeing yourself as inventive, happy, grateful for your creative nature.
- Keep a Journal. Writing about your dreams and goals makes them more real and signals to the subconscious mind that you are serious about change. The process of writing creates greater commitment. You should be sure to include any non-practical ideas and goals. That is, do not omit things that you think cannot come true. By judging hope and creativity as non-practical, you stifle yourself. Include practical steps to explore creative interests.
- Prioritize Activities. You can always find the time to do the things that are important to you. If you have time to sit and read a newspaper, a magazine, or watch a television show, you have some time available to devote to creative projects.

- Find balance. A balanced life restores your energy and allows for even more inspiration. Excessive work results in imbalance. If you have a demanding work schedule, you will need to relax or unwind after the busy-ness of activities. This is necessary. Too often, however, you may go from excessive activity to excessive loafing.

You have surely heard the term "workaholic." Do you have these tendencies? If so, think about the consequences to your life and happiness. Preoccupation with work, without inner exploration of one's self, and failure to prioritize meaningful relationships, will produce one-sidedness and disharmony.

You more easily become attached to your roles when you identify with the Limited Self, which has no sense of self beyond the parameters of worldly and role-related activities. This is how the small self perceives, measures and presents itself. The Eternal Self, on the other hand, does not identify with roles. It is pure being, pure consciousness. If locked into the smallness of the Limited Self, your awareness becomes narrower. You don't feel inspired to explore your inner being.

Embarking on the journey of discovering yourself as a creative being is a vital step towards further alignment between the two selves and tapping into the creative aspect of all life and all creation.

Journaling as a Creative Tool

As mentioned elsewhere, journaling is the technique of writing down your thoughts and feelings without censoring your ideas. It involves allowing free-flowing thoughts, emotions and ideas to be what they are, unhindered. Ideas, thoughts, and grammar are not to be arranged and edited with a reader in mind. Such free writing will give you greater clarity about yourself and lead to meaningful self-dialogue.

Keeping a journal handy makes it easier to develop the habit of writing down thoughts upon awakening or retiring. It is important to have a time for self-reflection at least twice a day for 15-20 minutes. It is in this free flow writing process that the consciousness becomes more transparent. Journaling is a wonderful tool of self-discovery and can increase your communication with yourself, allowing you to experiment with imagination and dreams: the dreams you live in the present and the dreams you long to express.

Journaling may also be used to clarify creative goals and map out the pathways to achieve them. To be successful, you begin by identifying and setting small, attainable goals with a projected timeline that is realistic. Then give yourself permission to begin. If you are interested in art, scheduling a time for yourself to walk around an art store is an excellent beginning. Another goal could be that you ask for information on a good book for a beginner. You may want to pursue information on classes or books and material available in an area that you have previously pursued. Develop strategies that make it feel more real to begin to investigate areas of interest. Some areas to explore when journaling:

a) List three areas of artistic or creative expression that you have wanted to try, expand, or revisit.

b) When considering new or past areas of creativity, what concerns, anxieties or fears come up for you? Fears of failure? Or are there fears about what would happen if you did succeed?

c) Is the thought of significant change frightening? Why? How would change interfere with your self-image? How does the idea of change impact your deservedness issues?

d) Are you able to give yourself permission to play with your creativity? Or are you fixated on the final outcome of your creative expression?

e) Have you had an idea or plan that you felt may have some practical value? Do you credit yourself as being someone who has creative ideas?

f) Do you have the idea for an invention or a modification of something that has already been marketed? Do you feel it might be worth pursuing any creative or inventive ideas?

g) List three areas in which you would like to express more creativity in the *practical* areas of your life, i.e., career, projects such as reorganizing home or office, or creative modification as a problem-solving tool.

h) Identify ways of approaching creative interests that would give you greater permission to explore. How can you give yourself permission to begin?

Becoming More Self-Aware

Journaling enhances introspection and improves the quality of your self-dialogue. You cannot change what you do not know. Journaling will allow you to visit your fears—both those that are known and those that lie deeper, buried in your unconscious. Writing can help to objectify areas of emotional difficulty and blockages that we all experience. This will give you a greater feeling of control over your life.

Do not underestimate the power of self-knowledge. You cannot uproot tenacious fear energy without first identifying it. As Socrates wrote, "The unexamined life is not worth living." By bringing the light of understanding to the "darkness" of your fears, you can see them and begin to release them.

If you do not explore your creativity, is the reason for this fear-based? If so, the first step in overcoming this fear is becoming aware of its presence and influence. Fear related to your creative energy may simply be due to the habit of self-negation or feelings of unworthiness. When you look at this tendency through a new lens of understanding, your broader perspective allows you to confront those issues more clearly, identifying their root causes and eliminating them from your life. Always keep in mind that habit patterns in consciousness may become your destiny. Every effort to bring them to light and to eradicate those that do not serve you brings you one step closer to freedom and creative self-expression. Consciousness, energy and manifestation are intrinsically linked.

By the use of imagination, permission to change, renewed intention and inspiration, you create a new destiny. May that new destiny contain more of your innate creative potential. The re-awakening of creativity presents keys that will open new doors of self-esteem and self-valuing. You gain more access to the truth of your own nature by the alignment of the Limited and Eternal Selves. With that increased merging, you tap into the dynamo of powerful creation itself. As you become more aware of the Creator within, you experience the Creator without. You are a dynamic, powerful creator, connected with the power of all creation.

Obstacles to Claiming Your Creative Self

If you look closely within, you will see that there are two main obstacles to accessing your creative self: the fear of failure and the fear of success. Behind most creative blocks is either one or the other. Many times one of these fears will manifest in the form of a paralyzing creative block that does not allow you to produce or achieve consistent follow-through with creative efforts. Sometimes you may choose

> *We pay a heavy price for our fear of failure. It is a powerful obstacle to growth. It assures the progressive narrowing of the personality and prevents exploration and experimentation. There is no learning without some difficulty and fumbling.*
>
> JOHN W. GARDNER

to do nothing rather than risk failure or success. This strategy often emerges to protect the self from others' judgments, assessments, and criticisms.

How you choose to participate in your own creativity is consistent with how your consciousness views your deservedness or worthiness. Fear proceeds from deep in the unconscious. You may be unaware of its cause. This is why journaling is vital. If you are to manifest your own special gifts and talents, it is essential that you uproot the causes of constrictions that prevent you from exploring your creative nature.

Fear of Failure

Fear of failure is something most of us, at some time or another, have experienced. This may be especially true when it comes to your creativity, for creativity involves exposing deeper parts of yourself. Expressing yourself may make you feel vulnerable.

As with the fear of success, the fear of failure can involve some level of psychological projection. What exactly is psychological projection? In Freudian psychology, *psychological projection* or *projection bias* is a defense mechanism. According to Wikipedia, it occurs when "a person unconsciously denies their own attributes, thoughts, and emotions, which are then ascribed to the outside world, such as to the weather, a tool, or to other people. Thus, it involves imagining or *projecting* that others have those feelings."

Said in another way, all that we perceive outside the self is a mirror of something within us. Everything that we see outside is a 'projection'. We project our energy, both positive and negative, onto other people and assume it is within them, often denying that it is within us. When we feel unworthy, at fault, or inadequate, we may keep those feelings unconscious, redirecting (or "projecting") them onto another.

Does this come into play with your fears around creativity? If you are not aware of your own internal dynamics, assumptions and projections, you can easily mislead yourself into thinking that there is "truth" in your lack of creative ability. You may assume that others do not find you capable, talented, filled with potential or worthy of success. This type of projection, an inaccurate assessment of yourself, can keep you locked in faulty self-definition.

Furthermore, if you received no validation or encouragement of your creative efforts as a child, you may have gone through life without a solid sense of self, afraid to take risks in creative expression. You may lack confidence and, having low self-esteem, you may project that others, too, have no faith in your abilities. This can turn into a self-fulfilling prophecy: you unconsciously create situations in which people do not support you so that you "validate" these feelings of unworthiness.

Early experiences of shame, embarrassment, and unworthiness, may have come throughout your life, triggered by events, relationships, or the inner movement of consciousness as unresolved issues surfaced. Fears of being exposed as untalented arise. Projection then validates your own faulty self-perception.

These themes of worthiness and deservedness are powerful and can subtly adopt various forms that show up as life obstacles. Assessing your own worth by the perceived opinions of others leaves you vulnerable and stuck in a cycle of helplessness. For many, the fear of failure thwarts, or can permanently thwart even minimal efforts at expressing creativity.

"In All Thy Getting, Get Understanding."

The good news is that your awareness of these principles alone can be liberating. Awareness is the birth of understanding. Journaling, along with the other practices described especially in the Stepping Stones to Change chapter of *Deliberate Happiness: The Complete Guide* can give you the power to stand firm in the face of fear and not be overwhelmed by it or succumb to a distorted perception of the self.

Part of the remedy when confronting fear of failure is the practice of self-dialogue and self-exploration. You have to remain ever mindful of the negative self-talk that echoes as loud chatter, berating and diminishing your own capabilities. Conscious attention to self-dialogue, and developing the habit of journaling to clarify mental processes, allows the creative process to expand. Such practices will also help you dissolve the shadows you cast upon your own creative process.

Your ultimate goal is to gain greater alignment with and integration of the Limited and Eternal Selves. The more you do this, the more your negative self talk will cease, and the less power the negativity of others will have over you. You will dramatically decrease your own struggles with worthiness and deservedness as you shift your identity to a much larger and more accurate assessment of yourself.

Regardless of your fears and struggles, change is always possible. Each effort you make on the path of life strengthens your confidence and self-knowing. If you have a solid enough sense of self, the opinions of others will not deter you from your creative endeavors. Failures will not devastate you. They may discourage you, surely, and you may be hurt by them, but you will not internalize them so deeply that they become your reality. Your natural urge to express your innate curiosity about life will propel you forward despite any lack of positive reinforcement. If you believe that you deserve good things to happen, you will take the risk to express your creative nature.

Often the desire to achieve public attention and fame from creative efforts is an expression of the need for love and approval that was not experienced in childhood. With sufficient admiration, you may assume that you will feel loved. But without self-validation and feelings of self-love, no audience will be sufficiently large to fill the internal void. Developing contentment within the self, and giving yourself permission to learn, explore and try new things without external approval are necessary to release the fear of failure.

Fear of Success

We can all relate to the fear of failure, but perhaps not so readily to the fear of success. If we take a deeper look at this fear, however, perhaps it, too, may have had an influence on your life.

Have you ever felt timid about exposing your talents or your deeper self to others? Have you ever entertained the thought that being successful might represent change, and that change might be painful? Would you open yourself more to others' criticism, rejection or ridicule? Any number of such thoughts and feelings may lie beneath the surface of your awareness, influencing or thwarting your efforts.

Perhaps you harbor an underlying fear that you are not worthy of success. If that fear exists, even unconsciously, you may feel safer remaining where you are and not trying something new. The core thought of being unworthy of success has enormous power. It may hide unrecognized behind thoughts such as: "Your success is a fluke. You will never be able to repeat this success or be applauded for your creativity again." Or "You know, you don't deserve the recognition. In the end, people will discover you are a fraud."

If you believe that success is a good thing, on the other hand, and that it won't hurt or alienate you from others, that you are, deep down, deserving of all good, then you won't be afraid or blocked.

Shifting the Cycle of Negativity

Ideas of unworthiness, feelings of inadequacy, and negative self-talk, underlie both fears of failure and fears of success. Negative self-talk constructs powerful walls that stifle and curtail the creativity within. From this day forward, affirm your creative nature. As you do, you will begin to pull down those walls. Give yourself full permission to step into a new level of creative expression.

STRATEGIES TO CONFRONT FEAR OF FAILURE OR SUCCESS:

- Increase positive self-dialogue and self-analysis.
- Analyze habit patterns of consciousness: As we think, so we create.
- Journal about fears related to both success and failure.
- Be willing to be a beginner.
- Focus on the journey; avoid preoccupation with the outcome.
- Affirm the creative power within; intend to explore and expand it.
- Experiment with, or learn, new areas of interest.
- Schedule time for creativity.
- Exercise imagination by allowing creative inspiration to flow.
- Give thanks in affirmations for the unfolding of divine creativity.
- Practice meditation. Emphasize Aum technique of Self-Realization Fellowship (available through a home-study course, Self-Realization Fellowship; 3880 San Rafael Avenue; Los Angeles, California 90065-3219.)
- Visualize being involved in successful, creative endeavors.
- Mentally give thanks for this creative aspect of life.
- Be creative in problem-solving and using inventive consciousness.
- Utilize positive visualizations as well as affirmations.
- Practice affirmations on creativity and worthiness to confront deservedness issues and invite the expansion of your creativity.

Creativity begins with small steps that are within reach. If you have always wanted to paint, for example, be willing to learn some basics in drawing or sketching. Try to learn the principles involved in depicting light, shadow and perspective from a book or a class. (An excellent book on art is *Drawing from the Right Side of Your Brain*, by Betty Edwards.) Or if you've always wanted to play or write music, be willing to learn the basics. Visualize yourself doing creative activities, feeling relaxed and successful.

Be willing to be a beginner! So many people lament that they are not masters of a particular artistic form. But all true masters in any field started as beginners. There is no shame in having no previous experience. There is, however, great sadness in not giving yourself permission to try.

Throughout this book you will notice references to the importance of giving yourself permission to change. Underneath this permission is the faith that you *can* change and that the Universe will *support* you when you try. Once given, that permission will open your creativity in ways that are boundless, limitless. Simply giving yourself permission will move your life and your energy with inspiration and imagination along new lines of creativity.

Finding Your Creative Pulse – A Visualization

Begin by breathing deeply. Deep breathing relaxes the mind and body and provides more oxygen to the brain for clearer thought and higher creativity. Always come back to your breathing. Is it shallow, or are you breathing freely? Ask yourself: "*What would I really love to do?*" or "*What have I been longing to do—for years?*" Dare to imagine your new possibilities. Your passion is a guiding light—showing you bright new possibilities in your personal and professional life.

Imagine yourself being given one wish that is guaranteed to come true. If you could do anything in the world, and if success

> *The spiritual law of reciprocity determines that what we give out returns to us. If we give out goodness, goodness will return to us and vice versa.*

were assured, what would you do? Let your consciousness roam in the limitless sea of possibilities. Follow the impulses of your heart and soul. Would you be a dancer? A pianist? A clothing designer? An inventor? Allow your imagination to explore the things you have always felt drawn to—your favorite colors, for example, or a beautiful garden setting. Be free to connect with whatever it is that most inspires your passion and interest.

During this exercise, project any images that come onto the movie screen of your imagination, focusing at the point between the eyebrows as if it were that screen. Begin the art of imagining and casting your desires into light forms of possibility. Focusing your attention with intention will stir your energy. Dynamic will energizes the scenes you imagined. Your mind can create what is now unimaginable. Your mind will etch creation into form. You are a creator!

Once your desires begin to manifest, make certain that they are aligned with spiritual principle. To gratify the self at the expense or detriment of others is not aligned with spiritual principle. Others have a right to their wants, needs, and desires. When you project your dreams, be certain that they will not be harmful, even unintentionally, to others.

> *Let your mind start a journey through a strange new world. Leave all thoughts of the world you knew before. Let your soul take you where you long to be…Close your eyes. Let your spirit start to soar and you'll live as you've never lived before.*
>
> ERICH FROMM

Remember, the Limited Self can create energized attachment to the ideas and scenes it visualizes, so exercise discernment. Attachment to your desires also sends the Limited Self into another level, a flurry of activity that intensifies the desires, actions, and activities well-grounded in ego-based consciousness. This, then, diminishes your awareness of the Eternal Self. The desired objects, or experiences, become identified in your mind as being the source of your happiness. If this occurs, you lessen your desire to focus on greater integration with the Eternal Self.

The Joy is in the Journey

The joy is in the journey, not the destination. Happiness comes from reaching out to your dreams, tapping into your deepest heart and allowing life to fully express itself. If you believe that joy will only come to you if you have achieved a final destination, you will have minimized the journey. And it is in the journey that you expend your life energy and creativity and become a new force of creation. Joy results from attending to your consciousness at this moment in time. If you focus sufficient attention on attending to your consciousness, you will penetrate from the outer fabric of life into the innermost domain of Being. In doing so, you touch the Eternal Now and your nature is transformed.

Becoming preoccupied with the end product of the creative adventure robs you of pleasure in that process and can intensify fear of failure or success in the pursuit of creative endeavors. See your efforts as a gift of your time and energy to the universe. As Lord Krishna counsels in the *Bhagavad Gita*, "Do not attach to the results."

When you become preoccupied with the end result, the self-critical voice constricts creative flow. Say mentally or out loud:

> *I give this gift of my time, energy and effort to the universe.*
> *I am aligned with my creative force and power.*
> *Creative energy is flowing and expressing through me.*

By placing your consciousness in the present moment, you align the Limited Self with the Eternal Self. The Limited Self darts between time sequences, as well as past and future events. Seldom, if ever, does the ego-driven, Limited Self, experience stillness in the now. Creativity is born in those moments of the now, not in the past or the future.

When you are absorbed in creative effort, the world stops. You are, for those moments, outside of time, in the flow, living in the Eternal Now. The act of creation stops the push and pull of polarity and you experience the vastness of your creative self. You experience the stirring of Spirit itself. In that process the two selves align. And in that greater alignment you draw closer to the face of God and to the mirror-reflection of your own divine nature.

Conclusion

You possess within your true nature a forceful creative dynamo that desires expression. That force wishes to be a co-participant with the divine Creator. When you were created, your consciousness was imbued with the principle of creativity. The very atoms of light danced into form. You are the power of that dream of Spirit. The stirring of imagination and thought energized into form underpins the expression of your being and your creativity.

You came into being by divine intention and the stirring of possibility. You, too, have the ability to stir creation into magnificent forms and dynamic images of infinite and varied possibilities. Be willing to dream your dreams. Blow breath into your dreams. Give your imagination the power of movement. Creation flows from your use of arrow-directed dynamic will, an electrified force field shimmering with every dream that could ever be entertained. Celebrate the inexhaustible possibilities! Go beyond any limiting ideas that diminish your life or the lives of others. Affirm your truth in order to claim your energy. The absolute power of creation resides within you. Tapping into and dynamically expressing that creative force is your birthright.

You were born out of the vision of God. The Creator of all instilled within you the power of creativity. The keys to the universe were placed in your hands and your right to the throne of creation was given to you as heir apparent. To bemoan your lack of talent or vision and your power as a creator is to denounce creation itself. Universes of possibilities move within you just as the heavenly bodies are rotating in divine perfection in deep space. May you capture the heavenly energy within and cast it into form.

True humility means to claim your oneness as a spark of that great overarching Spirit that is within all things. It means to accept what you have been given, The Gift of You.

The Gift of You

You are condensed starlight,
the sun and the moon of the universe.
You are a creator of divine sparks and emanations.
You are a carrier of the keys to the universe.
In your touch, hope awakens.
In your words, the sun shines brighter.
In your prayers, the moon softens the night.
And in your living, all the stars shine,
awakened from their sleep by your desires for knowing
and because you are.

To deny your Source or your abilities is neither humility nor accuracy of perception. The divine force of the universe has created you so that one day you will confidently claim your truth by penetrating into your light nature. You will feel the power within moving in joyous expression of self-knowing. All empowerment expresses true self-claiming. You will know yourself as Spirit moving in creation, unbounded by the flesh and the limitations of the world. You will know yourself as awake and alive in the Eternal Present! Your inspiration, imagination and flight with Spirit gives you universes to travel, wings to fly, and solar systems to explore.

Affirmations for Creativity

For Abundance through Creativity
Abundance and prosperity
are manifesting
through my creative endeavors
of will,
imagination,
and dynamic intention.

For Dynamic Co-creating
I am an instrument
of divine creativity.
I am a dynamic co-creator
with the universe.
Expansive, creative energy
is manifesting from me Now.

For Focus to Manifest Creativity
Night and day,
I am focused
in concentration.
My one-pointed focus
illumines all solutions
and dissolves all problems.
The power to create
is my birthright
manifesting.

For Creative Power in the Light
I am the Light
of all suns.
I possess the power
of all creations.
My name is the name
of all Light,
all suns,
all power,
and all creations.

For Infinite Creative Possibilities
Abundance
and ever-new creativity
are mine Now,
expressing with infinite possibilities.

Blessings Abound
I contemplate.
I see and penetrate
into unceasing
and unending
blessings.
I bow in gratitude
and appreciation.
I stand tall
In accepting all blessings.

BROWN VASE FLORAL

By Yvonne G. Christenson

CHAPTER TWO

ALIGNING YOUR DUAL NATURES: LIMITED SELF AND ETERNAL SELF

You are invited to embark on an adventure to expand your self-knowing and to practice spiritual techniques that will align your finite and Divine selves in the ultimate union, which is sustained happiness and joy.

KEY TOPICS ADDRESSED IN THIS CHAPTER:
- The art of happiness: not what you find, but what you create.
- Your entitlement to more happiness.
- Self-exploration and journaling as a technique.
- Preconceptions about happiness.
- Ideas that limit your access to more happiness.
- Self-knowledge and awareness of your spiritual essence.
- Hidden happiness contracts.
- Happiness in terms of a deeper relationship with yourself.
- Changing consciousness to change your circumstances.
- Introduction and exploration of the Limited Self.
- Introduction and exploration of the Eternal Self.

- Eternal Self's natural state of happiness and joy.
- Spiritual practices to align and integrate the two selves.
- Meditation, a basic technique.

The Essence of Happiness and Joy

The subject of happiness is so profound that it is written about in the world's great literature as well as in its eminent spiritual traditions. The pursuit of happiness is a fundamental right, referenced in the U.S. Constitution. It is a driving force that underlies our ventures and adventures in this physical world. Happiness also can be intensely consuming and powerful in and of itself.

But why do we pursue happiness? Why do you? Is it simply a reflex to avoid pain, or is it a distinct drive to access a greater, higher state of pleasure? Is pleasure simply experienced at the physical and psychological levels, or could there be a state of transcendent pleasure that is tied to our spiritual nature?

In this chapter I invite you to reflect on the nature of true happiness, to challenge self-defeating ideas and to understand that the key to igniting your creativity and manifesting abundance and prosperity comes in understanding that are two selves, an Eternal being of infinite light and love and a Limited self living in the material world of ego drives. Spiritual practices will help you to align and integrate those two selves.

The need for happiness seems so basic, so deeply intrinsic to our natures, yet it remains elusive. Our efforts to "find" happiness are usually misplaced, and we "find" only transitory happiness on the material level—a vanishing specter of possibility. But when we come to understand our dual natures, human and divine, and then experience and integrate them, we can begin to experience self-empowerment and then lasting happiness, and finally joy, our native state.

So for you, as for all of us, your dilemma is that you possess those two selves; they are in frequent communication, yet function in nearly opposite ways. This is not an abstract philosophical quandary; it is a pervasive reality. If you are not consciously aware of these two selves, your attempts to achieve peace, harmony, and happiness become more complicated. Yet mankind's deepest expressions of philosophical and religious thought often refer to this internal duality. Present-day author and psychologist John Welwood puts it succinctly: "To discover our human wholeness….we need to bring the two sides of our nature— absolute and relative, supra-personal and personal, heaven and earth— together at last." This integration offers hope for healing the schism and finding inner peace and happiness.

The Two Selves Defined

Let us take a deeper look at these two selves and how they operate in a polarized consciousness. For the sake of this discussion, let's call one self the Limited Self, identified and bound by the physical form, mind, feelings and the culture in which it lives. The other, the Eternal Self, expresses our spiritual nature, our true unchangeable essence.

> *Awakening is when the eyes of consciousness open so that consciousness begins to see what is real, instead of consciousness seeing only an illusion, or what it wants to be real.*
>
> JOHN DE RUITER
> *Dialogues with Emerging Spiritual Teachers*

Put simply, the Limited Self consists of:

- Your chemical, biological nature, operating in the physical dimension under physiological laws.

- Your psychological layers of mental consciousness, operating within a social context.

- Your beliefs and life experiences, operating within your environment and culture.

- Your extraordinary ability to evaluate, interpret and assign meaning to your experiences, literally defining yourself through your imagination.

Because we seldom view the interface between these four aspects, our Limited Self may feel compartmentalized, incorrectly interpreting experiences and events, wrongly imagining ourselves as body identified, continuously changing, impermanent beings.

Even though the Limited Self is unaware of its spiritual potential, it nonetheless carries the capacity for joy within. However, fragmentation, conflict, and persistent habits of thought—including the habit of worry, circular negative thinking and defeating self-talk—become impediments on the road to happiness and self-awareness.

> *The inner battle is between our lower self, or pseudo-self—the body identified ego—and our true higher self, the soul, the image of God within us.*
>
> PARAMAHANSA YOGANANDA

Your other self, the expansive Eternal Self, is your true spiritual nature, pursuing nothing, for its state of consciousness is joy transcendent. That Self, your soul nature, is always aware of the actions and activities of the Limited Self; your soul is the watcher over your ego. And this spiritual essence can manifest in subtle, powerful ways as the expression of who you truly are.

All physical life contains the movement of Divine Intelligence through the vibratory law of creation. As humans, we have an innate capacity to unfold through developmental stages into multi-faceted beings with highly advanced, complex thoughts, vivid imaginations, sparks of divine creativity and the ability to plan and achieve goals. Part of the miracle of our lives is that our magnificence in this form will never come again in exactly the same place, in the same way. Each of us is unique in the Universe. YOUR individual expression is unlike anyone else's.

Unfortunately, we generally go about life unaware of our infinite potential, for we are focused primarily on three-dimensional reality. We access knowledge through our bio-chemical nature and filter experiences through the individual persona, or ego. The five senses, as necessary as they are in helping us navigate this physical dimension, are like a twelve- inch ruler. They can measure the "fiber and texture" of the material world, but they cannot reach or measure Infinity.

Relentless forces of change assault this Limited Self, for nothing stays the same in this world. Even the semi-permanent values and mores of society are in a constant state of flux. As the world spins around us in an ever-changing panorama of experiences, our lives are impacted in ways great and small. Events happen, and we interpret and assign meaning to them. This capacity adds both to the wonder and the complexity to life. More often than not, our interpretation of events is subjective. Fundamentally, we place a fog—a kind of conceptual overlay—onto our experiences and then make an emotional investment in that overlay, taking it to be "real" in and of itself.

But all of us also have an innate ability to reflect on ourselves, a trait that lends resilience to us because our ability to interpret and imagine can open a door to new interpretation and redefinition. We can restructure the meaning we see in the physical dimension. "Consciousness is imaginative, sensitive and pliable; it can think and dream itself into any state," wrote Indian scholar and sage, Paramahansa Yogananda. He is referring here to our amazing ability to re-create ourselves, to change and transform consciousness itself.

While the capacity for self-motivated change is always present, the Limited Self is more often changed by biological or psychological conditions that continually impact it. It is altered by the hands of circumstances and the clay of environment: childhood and our early upbringing, genetics, and diet are just a few of the influences that continually impact this Limited Self. With such a constant bombardment of uncertainty, where there is really no telling what may happen in the next moment, is it any wonder that the Limited Self feels powerless against the law of change?

Stranger O' Self

Stranger o' Self
Dream Self gone wandering
Among the ruins of time
Gone to find self meeting self
Yet strangers always.

Stranger o' Self
Viewed from countless mirrors
Reflectors of false images
Self seeing self
Distorted on a mirror of glass.

Unknown substance
in search of form.
Stranger, Dream Self
Gone wandering
Among the ruins of time.

To operate entirely from the Limited Self makes the pursuit of happiness a precarious journey. "The only constant, is change," wrote the Greek philosopher Heraclitus. We do indeed live largely in a world of unending change over which none of us has true control.

But even when we assess ourselves through this limited, changeable self, we can continue to define, redefine and interpret. In my counseling work through the years, I have seen clients who awaken to their intrinsic capacity to choose new perspectives, and then are able to reframe even the most difficult memories and experiences. This is a profound truth that will be reinforced throughout this book.

Until we claim that power to choose, and until that choosing comes from our more enlightened, expanded Eternal Self, our perceptions will be constrained by the Limited Self's view of reality. What we see, hear, sense, feel and therefore experience, is filtered through the mind with all its pre-conditioning.

> *Happiness is inherent in oneself and is not due to external causes. One must realize one's Self in order to open the store of unalloyed happiness.*
>
> RAMANA MAHARSHI

We begin to believe our thoughts and perceptions are real, regardless of their origin. Roger Walse, in his "State of the Integral Enterprise: Part 1," wrote: "What is crucial to recognize is that all perceptions reflect perspectives, and all perspectives are partial and selective. Each perspective both reveals and conceals, clarifies and distorts. However, perspectives and perceptions do not clearly reveal their own limitations."

Assumptions and perceptions can harden into beliefs, which can manifest, consciously or unconsciously, as behaviors. It is imperative, therefore, that we learn to recognize how this process of self-definition operates.

As long as limiting beliefs remain unknown and unconscious, we remain a puppet, pulled by the strings of conditioned behaviors or false concepts of ourselves. As a result, we will continue to experience a limited range of happiness. Fortunately, at our best, we naturally strive to go beyond such limits; we want to experience ourselves as integrated and whole.

Personality is Ego-driven

Our personality, as delightful and creative as it may be, is limited to the perceptions of mind and body alone. Its drives are primarily based on preservation, survival, the elimination of pain, finding pleasure, and satisfying the senses, none of which, as we have seen, can provide true happiness. Nature intended for the ego-based personality to survive, reproduce, and endure. The emphasis of this ego-based personality is thus always upon the "I," which has little capacity to extend beyond itself to the needs, the necessities, the wants and desires of others.

Our human experience creates a kind of hypnosis in which we identify with the Limited Self. Jean Paul Sartre, the French existentialist, wrote: "Everything happens as if consciousness were hypnotized by this ego which it has established, which it has constructed, becoming absorbed in it as if to make the ego its guardian and law."

With this myopic view, the ego rarely sees beyond itself. Generally, the activities and drives of this ego-based personality do not allow for the stillness in which we can hear the call of the vastly subtler self. That other self, our soul nature, is ever in residence as we live in our physical-material reality. This self is hidden by the noise and drives of the world and our lack of attention to its existence.

Our Developmental Stages

Our entry into the material world as infants is driven foremost by the survival instinct. From this beginning, the infant embarks on a journey of growing and expressing increased mastery of its biology. The developmental progression from birth at a physical and psychological level has definite patterns and transitions. Certain milestones of development that are age specific must occur if there is to be a normal physical and psychological growth and maturation.

Renowned psychoanalyst, Erik Erikson, addressed specifically the developmental stages and the areas of attempted psychological mastery that must occur in those specific stages. Piaget's classic work on children also shows us stages of child development using copious research, observation, and journey metaphors; he reveals this development through the eyes of the child, providing a clear view of the Limited Self's necessary dominance in young human consciousness.

If a child grows with the proper guidance, developmental stages occur in proper sequence. These

> *What really has to (go) is our false self created by our own mind, ego, and culture. It is a pretense, a bogus identity, a passing fad, a psychological construct that gets in the way of who we are and always were.... This is the objective and metaphysical True Self.*
>
> RICHARD ROHR

stages, however, are influenced by the interaction of parents, significant others, and the community in which the child lives. Through words, example and behaviors powerful messages are delivered to the child: these contribute to his own self-identification. The child receives both overt and covert messages that have enormous potential for interpretation, and thus add to the intrigue and complexity of the youth's emotional and psychological journey.

The Limited Self is naturally rooted in this journey involving the physiological wiring of our nature in a physical world. By necessity, the child focuses on gaining greater skill over specific need areas, body mastery, and physical navigation in the world. This leads to body-based self-identification.

No wonder our self-esteem is reinforced by the idea that external mastery in the physical world is a natural source of happiness. So many messages in society reinforce this. Athletes become heroes; fashion models are idolized. Popularity is often based on glamour, wealth, and personality. Is it any wonder the young psyche can become confused?

The absorption and interpretation of messages, impressions, and ideas create an experience of self-identity There are not only layers

> *The ego feeling we are aware of now is…only a shrunken vestige of a far more extensive feeling – a feeling which embraced the universe and expressed an inseparable connection of the ego with the external world.*
>
> — SIGMUND FREUD

upon layers of experience, but also enmeshed layers of subtle reinforcement, and the co-mingling of these layers that create the masquerade of our "real self."

With the increasing capacity to contemplate, examine and verbalize one's experiences, the child feels that what we are calling the Limited Self is actually the core reality of his essence. Since the Limited Self must, of necessity, be identified with its biological journey and the physical, material world, it strives to access the world from this early core identification. The child seeks its happiness from the senses and the material world. Although the progressive formation of this Limited Self results in an undeniably real self, we are in truth, something vastly more complex, more wondrous.

Though most individuals abandon the ideas and desires of youth by changing or modifying them with experience, you may still claim this Limited Self as solid and enduring even though the frailty of that perception can be seen in the reflecting mirror of changing experiences. One of the great delusive ideas posits the solidity and permanence of the Limited Self amidst impermanence and fragmentation.

The more you bring these distorted, fragmented areas to conscious awareness, the greater will be the possibility of integrating them. The greater the denial about opposing parts within you, the greater the potential that you will experience conflict and lack personal integration. Denial and lack of self-knowledge perpetuate fragmentation and lessen your chances of experiencing continuous fulfillment and happiness.

Illusory Happiness

When asked to write down what you feel would give you happiness, you may naturally respond with answers centered on physical-material objects, or success in that realm. You may look to relationships or about love more generally for happiness. Someone else may believe that the possession of, or the constant access to, another person is the source of his or her happiness. This is because the Limited Self does not fully understand that the desire to experience love is also an invitation to know more of the Eternal Self. So instead, you may interpret love as a sensory or material experience associated with its own nature.

Happiness for the Limited Self has to be tied to the experiences or desires of life in a physical body in a material world. In this state of being, your capacity for happiness is not only determined by your habitual state of mind, whether positive or negative, but by your emotional response to events. Emotions become charged with expectation and interpretation. This generally leads to replaying and reinterpreting along similar ideas or themes. We all replay memories and interpret them yet again. And off we go on a repetitive cycle that is difficult to break. Let's take a deeper look at how such thought patterns work.

How Habit Patterns are Formed

Your interpretations of events create energy. This blueprint energy creates grooves in your brain that allow for further movement of energy through which your consciousness travels. New experiences tend to gravitate into existing energy grooves. Once a particular thought groove is activated by a repetitive thought, a tendency is formed. It is extremely difficult to change the tendencies of the physical mind for so many of your thoughts are automatic and therefore unconscious.

In the last few decades, scientists have shown that we can change the structure and function of our brains by the way we think. This newly conceptualized feature of the brain is called neuroplasticity. For years, the conventional wisdom of neuroscience held that the hardware of the brain is fixed and immutable – that you, like all of us, are stuck with what you were born with. Yet *Wall Street Journal* science writer, Sharon Begley, reveals an entirely new paradigm in her book, *Train the Mind, Change the Brain*. She describes pioneering experiments in the field of neuroplasticity that investigate how the brain can undergo wholesale change. These experiments reveal that the brain is capable not only of altering its structure but also of generating new neurons, even into old age.

By the act of mental repetition, and the mental replay of ideas, you create new energy grooves. Your power to create new energy grooves means that you have the power to recreate, re-imagine, and re-energize any event that occurred in the physical-material world.

You stand at a crossroads with every experience in life from smelling a flower to failing an exam at school, dealing with a promotion to falling in love or coping with a major loss. How you interpret the experience determines your reality and sets up the blueprint for similar experiences in the future. Your interpretive capacity crystallizes these perceptions in a manner that either integrates or fragments your self, creating harmony or dissonance. The repetition of these ideas forges self-identity and creates energy grooves and memory grooves in the physiology of the brain itself.

The repetition of these themes can lead to either positive or negative self-talk. The more you energize and repeat any theme, the greater and deeper are the energy grooves available for that theme. And the deeper and more pronounced the energy groove, the more likely that you will repeat the same interpretations. The late self-help author Robert Collier put it this way: "One comes to believe whatever one repeats to oneself sufficiently often, whether the statement be true or false. It comes to be the dominating thought in one's mind." It is imperative, therefore, that you become more aware of your habitual trends of thought.

Confusion can result when you place too much emphasis on your interpretations of events, experiences and interactions. These interpretations are simply the movement of energy in chemical, biological and energy fields. They are not the true reflectors of reality. The habit of repeating ideas may help you feel solid. You may mistake that "solidity" for who you truly are. Ultimately, that is an illusion. You are more than your biology, interpretations, emotions, and habits of thought!

Psychology and Self-Help

Most self-help books are based on the premise that to achieve happiness or peace, we must better understand and master our psychological underpinnings.

But it is *only* the Limited Self that can achieve greater self-understanding through psychological approaches to self-discovery. This is a worthy endeavor, of course, for introspection, self-examination, and self-analysis are helpful tools in the process of knowing ourselves. Psychology is about the journey of consciousness, addressing as well the physiological aspects of life and their impact on consciousness. But if the consciousness of the Limited Self becomes the only area of investigation, the discovery of a larger, spiritual Self will be sacrificed and with it, the attainment of true integration.

You need to find the middle path. Bypassing the Limited Self in your efforts to access your spiritual self will not bring freedom and happiness anymore than the reverse. Buried, denied and unresolved psychological issues will continue to fester and do damage if left unaddressed. Without deep inner work, those issues remain and will spring up as you move past the Limited Self to delve more deeply into your spiritual nature. John Welwood speaks to this truth in his *Toward a Psychology of Awakening:* "As awareness starts to move beyond the boundaries of the conditioned personality structure, this expansion inevitably challenges that structure, flushing out old, subconscious, reactive patterns that often emerge with a vengeance."

When these reactive patterns are flushed to the surface, psychology can be a helpful therapeutic tool. Psychological assistance from the hands of trained professionals can give you an invaluable gift, the gift of greater self knowledge and the possibility of understanding more of yourself, your journey, and the movement of your own consciousness. However, psychology in general has little value in the territory and the analysis of the spiritual nature of man. Any lasting transformation of your human consciousness ultimately has to provide the unshakable realization that you are at your core, a spiritual being, possessing an unchangeable nature rooted in joy.

Introducing the Eternal Self

Beyond the Limited Self is another Self, constant, changeless, integrated, unbounded by physiology, unaffected by alternating psychological states, impervious to societal or cultural influences. It functions by intuition, free of interpretation and faulty self-definition.

This Eternal Self is not searching for happiness because it already exists in the state of unalterable joy intrinsic to your very being. Your drive for happiness is not simply the thrust of your desire for self-gratification or for pleasure at a biological level. Rather, it is the spiritual call to a vision of yourself that may often be obscured by the seeming reality of the material world.

What if, in the search to discover who you are, you should find this expansive, radiant self underneath the layers of personality and material identifications? How would you experience it? Many of the world's spiritual traditions describe this self as the essence of Spirit, manifesting in creation through the vibratory energy of love and light. Though you may not consciously be aware of this self, it is nevertheless real and truly who you are. While you experience life as a physical being, this self remains profoundly separate, yet powerfully a part of us, immutable, unchangeable, enduring, permanent. This self is the expression of your soul nature. Here is a poem I wrote about this essential Self.

Forever More I Shall Be

I am
I am that which is
I am that which will always be.

I am immutable
I am the fortress
I am beyond all destruction.

I am deathless
I withstand all
For I am all.

When the world and the universe of matter
Shall crumble, I shall remain serene!
When the sun shall fall from the heavens
My light shall light the world of worlds!

When I shed forevermore my forms
I shall be with form
And yet formless!

For I am
And forever more I shall be!

The Eternal Self is Spirit participating in the journey of being human. If this is so, how, then, might you find greater happiness, especially if the essence of your being is already joy itself? Perhaps this joy is undiscovered, perhaps this peace is uncultivated, but nevertheless, in the purest sense, that eternal joy exists. And so the art of finding true happiness lies in accessing and empowering who you truly are, spiritual beings who are living a physical-material journey. Without the journey inward, you may find that lasting happiness is always just beyond your grasp. *This journey requires deep commitment to self-discovery, and steadfast patience, as the Irish saying goes, the "patience that can conquer destiny."*

THE WELL OF SILENCE WITHIN

Meditation has been used through the centuries as a method for acquiring spiritual self-knowledge. It is based on the idea that as the consciousness becomes interiorized, you have more access to your essence or true nature. "Be still and know that I am God" conveys this truth with simple clarity. The silence of meditation is not just a passive quietness. It embodies a dynamic and vast consciousness far beyond your usual experience. In this mental stillness, you can access your own hidden consciousness.

Real empowerment must include the cultivation of a relationship with your truest self, the Eternal Self, which rests in the center of your being. This Self begins to emerge when you peel away the layers of ego consciousness through meditation, introspection and other

> *Being is not only beyond but also deep within every form as its innermost invisible and indestructible essence. This means that it is accessible to you now as your own deepest self, your true nature....You can know it only when the mind is still. When you are present, when your attention is fully and intensely in the Now.*
>
> ECKART TOLLE

awareness-based practices. All beings, no matter how reactionary, fearful, violent or lost, can open themselves to the sacred within and become free. Spirit is your very being. Meditation allows you access to the deeper regions of your spiritual nature, connects you with the Divine presence within, and will provide you with a clearer vision of the truth. Scheduling time each day for meditation practice is essential not only for your peace and well being and empowerment, but also for experiencing your Eternal Self, the true source of lasting happiness. There are countless meditation techniques available and myriad philosophies about the proper method of meditation. Finding an effective and suitable style of meditation can take time and experimentation but will prove invaluable. One technique is offered below.

Meditation Technique

The proper posture for meditation is very important.

- Sitting in a straight back chair is recommended.
- The feet should be flat on the floor, pointed straight ahead.
- In a state of relaxation, maintain a straight spine, to the best of your ability without strain or discomfort.
- Place your hands, with palms turned gently upward, near the junction between your legs and thighs. (Note: Meditation techniques, in general, should not be practiced with the individual lying down in a bed. In this posture, the meditative state too easily becomes a sleep state. If an individual has the physical ability to sit either in a chair with feet flat on the floor—or cross-legged on the floor on a flat surface—the sitting posture should be assumed. In general avoid sitting on a bed, for consciousness usually associates the bed with sleep.)

This meditation technique involves focusing your attention at the point between the eyebrows known as the "spiritual eye." This is a center that increases your spiritual connectedness as you focus on it. If you are having difficulty in achieving or maintaining the proper eye position for your meditation, the following suggestion may assist you in getting the correct angle for your focus gaze. The eyes should be turned gently and slightly upward.

Pencil Technique for Proper Gaze

Visualize holding a #2 pencil eraser at the spiritual eye. Visualize the eraser resting on the forehead between and slightly above the eyebrows, with the pencil parallel to the ground. Allow your focus to move to where you visualize the point of the pencil to be. Keep the gaze focused at that spot. This technique is not part of the practice itself, but will prevent you from placing excessive strain on the eyes and help develop a better habit pattern for meditation.

Note: There should be no strain or tension. This is a natural, pleasant position for the eyes. If there is strain or tension, the gaze may be turned too far upward, or the eyes may be slightly crossed. Check the eye position.

Preparation for Meditation:

- Visualize that you are encircled by white light that either outlines the body or appears as a spherical egg-shape. Your <u>intention</u> to place white light around the body summons a greater connection with Spirit and strengthens the energy field.

- After visualizing the white light in this way, begin to observe the breath in a relaxed state of mind. Maintain the correct posture with spine erect and feet flat on the floor.

- Affirm that the surrounding white light of Spirit divinely protects you. (Example: "I am surrounded by the light field of the Divine. I am ever protected. I am ever embraced by the Divine Force.") Repeat this protection affirmation, or a similar one, five or six times.

- Now, in this relaxed state of mind, begin to observe the breath without any attempt to regulate it. Neither speed up nor slow down the rhythm of the breath. Simply observe the inhalation and exhalation as it naturally flows in and out.

- See yourself "piggy-backing" on each inhalation and exhalation. Mentally say, "I ride the inward breath." As you naturally begin to exhale, mentally say, "I ride the outward breath." Continue this pattern for approximately 15 minutes. Visualize yourself riding the inward breath and the outward breath. Then change the repetition of words on the inhaling and exhaling breath to "I am That[1]".

Additional affirmations that may be mentally repeated prior to or following the use of this meditation technique:

I ride the inward breath.
I ride the outward breath.
I am one with that breath.
Reveal Thyself.

Note: Effective meditation techniques are available from Self-Realization Fellowship in the form of lessons that are delivered to your home every two weeks.

---

[1] "I am That" refers to our being One with the Indwelling Spirit.

For information contact:

Self-Realization Fellowship
3880 San Rafael Drive
Los Angeles, CA 90065-3219
323-225-2471
http//www.yogananda-srf.org

Such techniques of will-charged visualization and spiritualized affirmation are also powerful conduits and conveyors of truth that promote access to this highest self. The irony is that your spiritual, expansive, all-knowing self is never in pursuit of its own happiness. Its nature is already joy, peace, and bliss. In its silence, the Eternal Self is summoning the Limited Self into a greater alignment with itself. In the Greek myth, Narcissus falls in love with his own image reflected in a still pool of water. In a spiritual interpretation, he may be seeing the truth of his own divine nature reflecting back to him in the still waters.

While this reflection is generally obscured, there is nevertheless a powerful drive within not only to perceive our true image, our true Self, but to become fully one with it. We desire the joy that is more than an extension of the happiness of the earth. Seemingly just out of reach, we tend to fall back on our belief in the tangible self of change and vacillating, unstable circumstances. You, too, may operate on the myth that this kaleidoscope of images is your true self and that if you can run fast enough, you will catch and possess yourself and achieve a state of unchanging happiness. Like the proverbial dog chasing its own tail, you may go round and round in search of something already within us.

True access lies in the stillness and the subtleties of the movement of Spirit. Eckart Tolle wrote: "Your innermost sense of self, of who you are, is inseparable from stillness. This is the I Am that is

Aligning Your Dual Natures: Limited Self and Eternal Self

deeper than name and form." His words are an invitation to you to embark on a voyage of self-discovery. They invite your activity-driven mind and sense identification to move past the pursuits of the world, toward calmness, serenity, peace, tranquility, and self-knowing beyond any definition. This is where deep meditation will take you.

If you believe that in time you will possess happiness because of the nature of your dreams and goals, the world offers strong encouragement to continue to pursue that pathway. Perhaps nothing that others say will alter the momentum of that journey. But if you doubt that the world in and of itself will be able to provide happiness, know that doubt itself can be a catalyst for you to go deeper, thus creating a bridge to a new level of integration between the two selves.

The tools of meditation, visualization and affirmation are the bridge-builders for the fragmented parts of your Limited Self. To achieve true, lasting happiness, the self of the world must come into alliance, alignment and attunement with the Divine aspect of the self.

Characteristics of the Limited Self and Eternal Self

Limited Self	Eternal Self
Ego-driven consciousness	Spirit-based consciousness
Identifies with the body and the material world	Not subject to identification with body, senses or material pleasures
Biological and psychological identification is foundational	Spirit in man beyond all definition and identification
Shaped by experiences and interpretations of those experiences	Immutable, absolute in Being regardless of experiences
Resides in our genetic heritage	Independent of genetic heritage
Desires to seek and possess happiness	Never in pursuit of its own happiness; continually joyful
Progresses through an innate developmental pattern of psychological and biological stages	Manifests in creation through the vibratory energy of love and light
Impacted and changed by circumstances and faulty self-definition	Not impacted by changing conditions or circumstances
Struggles with feelings of powerlessness against the Law of Change	Changeless nature is constant joy, peace, bliss
Ever changing and unstable due to circumstances, with illusion of control	Has enduring permanence, unfaltering truth, vibratory consistency with spirit
Happiness associated with fulfillment of biological drives and gratification	Happiness inherent in Being independent of external desires

Affirmations to Help Integrate Your Dual Nature

For Integration
Attuned, Aligned,
Integrated Self
Content in Being,
Peaceful in Serenity,
Awake in Spirit.

For Joy-filled Bliss
Being in knowing
I am
Joy-filled,
light-illuminated,
ever penetrated,
ever known.
Joy-filled bliss I am.
Joy-filled bliss I am.

For Becoming One with the Light
I am the Light
of all suns.
I possess the power
of all creations.
My name is the name
of all Light,
all suns,
all power,
and all creations.

For Seeing My Face in God
I behold the face of God.
I parted the curtains of penetration
and the face I saw
was my own.

For Becoming One with All That Is
In becoming one
with nature
I claim my
nature.
I am Spirit
in nature.

For Silent Discovery
In silence,
the seeker finds
himself.

For Intentional Focus
Intentioned focus increases my power
of concentration.
In concentration
I perceive the whole,
and the parts,
moving in perfected
harmony.

For Greater Purified Consciousness
Oh Lord, may I become less of myself
in ego-based consciousness
that I may become ever more one with Thee.
May I become truly a purified conduit
of Your love, of Your light, of Your grace.

For Becoming a Mirror of the Divine
May I become a perfected mirror
of the divine essence
which is You, Oh Lord.

ORANGE LIGHT
By Yvonne G. Christenson

CHAPTER THREE

Deservedness and How to Feel It

You are invited to the inner journey that affirms your worthiness, deservedness and entitlement to receive the gifts and grace of your divine nature. Your feelings of deservedness create or block the flow and manifestation of circumstances in your life. If you accept this sacred invitation and wish to change your circumstances, you must change your consciousness.

KEY TOPICS ADDRESSED IN THIS CHAPTER:
- Exploring your beliefs about your deservedness.
- Consciousness creates your circumstances.
- Assessing beliefs about your worthiness/deservedness to receive.
- Analyzing your self-dialogue.
- Affirming negative and positive statements.
- Origins of your sense of unworthiness.
- Steps in changing your self-concept.

- Methods of transforming negative self-talk: imagination, dynamic intention, and dynamic, will-charged affirmations.
- Helping to reclaim a sense of deservedness and entitlement.
- The struggle of the Limited Self.
- The power to limit or create via circular energy patterns.
- Shame, guilt, and the role of conscience.
- Inherent Spiritual Truth versus Indoctrination.
- Redemption from shame and guilt by the law of Grace.
- Why you are deserving and entitled.

Self-Exploration of Deservedness

The previous chapter on Creativity has shown that often the greatest obstacle to your full, oceanic expression of creativity can be your own sense of self-worth. In order to remove such obstacles, you must first explore your feelings about your right, deservedness, and worthiness to be a receiver of the good in your own life. As a child of God or a divine participant in the universe, do you feel you deserve at a deep core level to be happy, to receive the good including abundance and prosperity? Perhaps you feel you are deserving, but for some unknown reason you never had a chance to express your joy in the bounty of life, in the flow of love, in prosperity and happiness. Do you feel life passes you by, no matter how hard you try? And if so, do you perceive your difficulties as coming from bad luck, or do you think that some of your problems result from your own habits and repetitive thoughts? Perhaps you actually feel that others are luckier or more entitled to be happy, prosperous, and nurtured than you are.

Your feelings about your worthiness influence not only your role as a generator of possibilities, but also partially shape your relationship with the Divine. The science of psychology offers one valid perspective on happiness and self-esteem. Yet it is man's metaphysical dilemma that frequently hammers the core feeling about our right — and yours— to receive that greater good. Your own ideas of deservedness and your own self-definition dramatically thwart or support your relationship with Spirit and your pursuit of abundance, prosperity and happiness.

Whatever you believe you deserve, you project deeper into your feelings and patterns of emotion. If you harbor deep feelings that you are undeserving of receiving the good, those feelings may undermine your sincere and genuine efforts at change, including your spiritual techniques as well. You must get clear about the attitudes and habits of consciousness within you. The greater your feelings of unworthiness and lack of deservedness, the greater will be your resistance to systematically using techniques of change, including visualization, affirmation, and meditation. If you are to counter negative ideas, you must become more aware of your habitual thought patterns. Once you do that, you can gradually substitute negative, repetitive thoughts with positive, affirming affirmations.

Feelings of unworthiness always translate into some type of negative self-statement. This negative self-statement becomes a negative affirmation. These negative ideas then become projected themes around your self-identification. Any energized theme that directly, or indirectly, states your lack of entitlement becomes an affirmation. In a sense, the negative thought becomes a mantra of living, an energized thought form operating by the law of magnetism and attraction, like bringing forth like.

Such negative affirmations may be counteracted by the use of powerful positive affirmations proclaimed with dynamic intention of will.

Journey in Consciousness Exploration

We all have the power to negate ourselves as a creator and as a potent life and light force in the universe. We also all have the power to begin to create a new reality consistent with the innate harmony within ourselves, with others, with nature, and with Spirit. Shifting your consciousness from a role as victim to one as divine co-creator can unleash your power to create the positive instead. Answering the journaling and self-assessment questions that follow will help you make that shift, one that can eventually lead to a transformation of consciousness. But as you move through the exercises, providing honest answers, remember that any real, sustained change will likely involve consistency of effort and spiritual principles.

Introspection Opportunity

- What are the areas of your life that you would like to change?
- What are the areas in which you could experience greater success, reward, or happiness by increasing positive flow?
- List the areas in which you desire to see dramatic change, knowing change cannot occur without rooting out feelings of unworthiness.

Self-Assessment

- How do you assess your self-worth?
- Do you base your assessment on your possessions or status in the material world?
- Do you assess your worth based on meaningful relationships or deep moments of connection with others?
- Do you define your worth on the capacity to receive or to give? Or a combination of these attributes?
- Do you assess your worth and define who you are based on your personality traits and feedback from others?
- Or do you possess a deep place of self-knowing independent from societal values, impressions of others, or definitions of the

world? In that deep place, is there a part of you that feels you are more than you, yourself know? Is that self beyond the access of the perception of others and the definition of the world itself?

THE POWER OF YOUR SELF-ASSESSMENT

Honest replies to these further questions are key to your self-assessment:

- Do you feel entitled to receive, to benefit, and to extract good, abundance, peace, joy, and happiness in your life?
- Do you feel worthy to claim and take that profound journey tied to your innermost essence?
- Are you waiting to feel good enough, perfect enough, lovable enough, creative or talented enough, to claim more of yourself?

INTROSPECTION EXERCISE

Write five experiences, inspirations or events that have allowed you to progress or succeed in some aspect of your life.

Then write five events, episodes or repeated themes that impacted you, from your early life, in a negative way.

Having a clearer idea of the negative and positive ideas that have impacted your life may help you understand how you repeat themes about yourself in your internal dialogue. It may also give you an understanding of how those positive and negative experiences tend to repeat in the patterns of adult life.

- How does your spiritual perception of yourself equate with the way others define who you are?
- Do you see yourself as disconnected from Spirit, from God, or your own spiritual nature?
- Do you believe that you have a spiritual nature?

- In your spiritual assessment of yourself, are you more likely to view yourself as fallen, a sinner, or do you view yourself as a divine child of God?

- Do you feel unworthy to be recognized, honored, or part of a Higher Power?

- Do you have an expansive view of yourself aligned with spiritual truth?

- Do you expect change to happen as instant transformation and instant gratification?

In order to begin visualizing positive change for yourself, write down what you feel your circumstances or conditions will be in one year, three years, five years, and ten years. Analyze what things you put on the list. Do you see yourself as initiating and having power over the changes or do you see such results a being a recipient of good fortune and opportunities from others? Or perhaps both?

If you, at a deep level, feel that you are unworthy, or that you do not deserve to be loved, or to be prosperous, successful, or to be spiritual, again you will find those manifestations originated from your thought, the origin of ideas. Neutral thoughts have minimal energy. Energized thought, whether negative or positive, creates your material circumstances. What you say to yourself becomes truth, whether or not it has any basis or substance in fact.

The unconscious mind will not evaluate the truth of a statement; it will operate as if all statements are true. You must be very careful what you say about yourself and what you affirm to be true. For instance, if you have experienced a failure around a particular project or endeavor, do you state the project or endeavor "failed," or do you state, "I am a failure"? Do you see the setback as tied to a particular situation or circumstance, or do you state it in a way that defines you? The repetition of such thoughts as, "I am a failure" or, "My good ideas never succeed," will continue to create a dynamic flow in direct opposition to that which you desire. When you personalize negative ideas into statements about yourself, you create negative dialogue and life themes that constrict the flow of positive, dynamic energy. Constricted energy inhibits personal expansion, belief in self, and your ability to access your true powers.

Some self-help books and popular psychologists recommend simple visualization techniques as magical tools for manifesting your deepest desires. Alluring as these sound in their seeming effortlessness, simple visualization techniques are limited unless accompanied by efforts towards deeper, internalized changes in consciousness. Will-directed intention, projected with affirming truths, on the other hand, can create sustained changes in consciousness, circumstances, and manifestation.

A sense of worthiness, entitlement, and deservedness, must be stated and restated, fortified by the intention of focused will and concentration in order to develop a sufficient force field of the positive. This is necessary to counter negative self-talk. If like is to attract like, you must become a generator of the positive and must be able to state the truth of your right to pursue, express and possess happiness, peace, serenity, well-being, and spiritual awareness. You <u>are</u> entitled to happiness! You are entitled to be a receiver of the good! You are a powerful co-creator with the universe, summoning the light of universes!

INTROSPECTION OPPORTUNITY

Assess your beliefs about your worthiness and deservedness by using this scale, from 1 to 5, with 5 indicating strong feelings of worthiness and deservedness, and 1 indicating feelings of unworthiness and lack.

1. Do you feel you are deserving or worthy of being loved? Rate yourself on a scale of 1-5.
2. Do you feel you deserve or are worthy to participate in abundance and prosperity? Rate yourself on a scale of 1-5.

3. In the area of health and wellbeing, do you feel you deserve greater health and wellness? Do you feel you deserve to be ill because of previous life choices? Rate those on the scale of 1-5.

4. Do you feel you deserve happiness and success that involves expressing creativity? Do you feel you are worthy of considering yourself a creative, inspired individual? Also on a scale 1-5.

5. Do you feel you are entitled to a higher level of relationship with yourself, the universe, or God? Do you make statements such as, I am "unworthy," "not good enough," or "spiritually undeserving"?

In order to determine whether early issues continue to limit the flow of good in your life, you must pay close attention to the pattern of negative self-statements that you make in times of stress or crisis. What do you say to yourself when something negative happens? What is the pattern of those thought processes? Ask yourself whether, in the area of of love, you repeat ideas or statements that you are not truly good enough to be loved. Perhaps you secretly believe that your relationships are doomed to failure. Perhaps you have resigned yourself to a state of mediocrity. If so you are probably making statements about your limitations in prospering and in achieving true abundance, prosperity and a greater flow in all areas of life.

Analyzing Your Self-Dialogue: Destroy the Negative, Create the Positive

With persistence and focus, you will be able to expand your awareness of your thought patterns, analyze repetitive themes of the mind and emotions, listen to and write down the negative self-statements you make. Becoming more familiar with your own patterns of negative self-talk will empower you to make changes. You can become an energy magnet by using positive self-talk and visualizing positive circumstances. If you perceive those events as external and independent from the movement of your consciousness, you may find it difficult to persist in efforts to analyze your consciousness and bring about change. Replaying and analyzing your thought patterns throughout the day will give you a clear indication of how much time you focus on negative self-themes or positive affirming self-statements.

Write down those themes; estimate the mental time spent around negative self-ideas and around positive self-ideas. Your self-dialogue is powerful because you are supplying to those ideas the energy of creation to begin a true process of materialization and manifestation. The power of the Creator is within you. The powerhouse of universal energy is within you. Your being is charged with a thousand suns of possibilities and your mind can be the sculptor of present and future manifestation in your life. You have the power! What ideas are revolving in your consciousness as you use this powerful mind source to create?

You Are Entitled to Change and to Receive

> *Our deepest fear is not that we are inadequate. Our deepest fear is that we are powerful beyond measure. It is our light, not our darkness that most frightens us. We ask ourselves, Who am I to be brilliant, gorgeous, talented? Actually who are you not to be? You are a child of God. Your playing small does not serve the world...We were born to make manifest the glory of God that is within us, not just in some of us, but in everyone.*
>
> — MARIANNE WILLIAMSON

- **Analyze and identify your mental habits** and thought processes to identify those patterns that need to be changed.
- **Internalize the truth** that mental repetition of ideas does not equate with truth or validity.
- **Use will-based intention** in order for change to occur.
- **Increase the positive thoughts** and statements about life, others, and yourself by identifying those habits of thought.
- **Strengthen the habit pattern of more positive thoughts**.
- **Decrease negative thoughts** and statements about life, others, and yourself by identifying those mental patterns.
- **Use spirit-based affirmations systematically** to create vibrational shifts that can truly transform consciousness over time.
- **Proceed with affirmations and positive visualization**, even if you do not believe anything will change.

Know that replacing negative ideas with positive, powerful, spirit-affirming statements can generate positive shifts. These shifts alter consciousness and can directly manifest positive changes in circumstances. These shifts can occur whether or not you believe those thoughts are true, real, believable, or possible.

- **Affirm positive change NOW.** (Thoughts have the power to blueprint the future and change the NOW.)
- **Increase your spiritual participation in life**. Pursue that which is deep and meaningful for your life. Be cautious of any organization or group that asks you to transfer your personal power or assets and denies your own capacity to access the highest aspects of yourself or God.

It's important to understand that your deep-seated sense of deservedness or unworthiness has complex origins based on:

- Childhood experiences and interpretations of those experiences.
- Internalized values.
- Circular negative feelings.
- Negative self-talk.
- Shame and guilt, a shroud of shame dulling the bright light of God within.

Childhood Experiences

Childhood themes imprint powerfully. In developmental stages throughout childhood we harness streams of imaginative energy and the power of self-definition to achieve amazing mastery, skill, and abilities. In addition to such achievements, we also have internalize negative ideas, messages, and themes. Imagination not only plays a role in interpreting the events that happen to you, but your imagination projects thoughts about how others see you. Imagination is the artist's brush by which your self-image is formed. Negative self-talk is a prevalent and destructive result of the improper use of imagination and faulty interpretation of experiences and encounters with others.

Where Did Any Negative Self-Talk Begin?

How did the negative themes develop?

1. Negative experiences may occur at early, impressionable ages.
2. Opinions or behaviors may come from our parents, or significant others, in our childhood—the events that actually occurred.

3. Perceptions about what occurred can include real and imagined impressions of childhood messages.

4. Repetition of ideas about these experiences and perceptions can expand them into persistent self-negating themes for the adult. Ideas become themes.

5. Your continuing self-assessment, self-measurement, and self-talk reinforces these self-negating themes, and replays them based on your earlier imaginative, interpretive experiences.

6. Negatively-interpreted experiences may emerge from school or community events.

7. Childhood trauma that involves abuse and/or violations of trust usually results in self-negating talk and shame.

8. Disruption of early developmental stages, usually the result of emotional or physical neglect or adult disconnection, can breed negative themes about the self.

9. Other sources of negativity include physical or emotional abandonment such as death, divorce, or absence of a significant other in the life of a child.

The child may become handicapped, not only by the experiences of childhood, but by the interpretations of the experiences that occurred at impressionable ages. Perceptions then become energized thought forms.

Early social values internalized in childhood are rooted in such experience and interpretations, but are also influenced by the society in which you were born. Socio-economic values and religious and political views have a sociological backdrop. Messages from the family and significant others and the community intermingle with the existing family structure. Ideas, philosophies, and values are absorbed as you become acculturated. Internalized messages become part of your consciousness.

Children may be psychologically harmed in many ways, including abuse, excessive authoritarian control, minimal positive interaction, emotional neglect, inadequate adult role models. The dysfunction of adults may damage children in ways that make them more susceptible to dysfunction in their adulthood, including problems such as substance abuse, mental illness, or impaired capacity to relate to others.

Early experiences, mentally replayed in your mind, can develop into a pattern of negative self-talk. This negative self-talk shapes early self-identity and self-definition that has the power to carry into adulthood. Who are you really? Are you separate from who you believe yourself to be? Or are you defined by your own powerful, repetitive self-definition, including negative self-talk?

Children often feel that they are the reason adults mistreated, neglected, ignored, abandoned, or abused them. They do not understand the adult psyche, their own psyche, or the adult world. They have no capacity to grasp the psychological issues, or family dynamics of the parents, or others, in their lives.

Because of their inability to grasp the larger picture, children always pull events back to themselves, as if the mistreatment springs from their own psyche, behavior, or self-concept. Children blame themselves. And this belief that they are to blame for neglect, adult emotional or mental disconnection, death, abandonment, trust violations, and various forms of abuse has no basis in truth. The child believes powerfully that bad things would not have occurred had they been "good enough."

Children, seeing themselves as the source of trouble in the family, begin to create a foundation of self-negation and low self-esteem. Feelings of unworthiness, and deep core feelings of being undeserving, as well as a sense of spiritual dislocation are all part of self-negation.

Continual criticism by parents about the core of the child create great difficulties in developing positive self-worth and self-esteem.

By contrast, parental strategies that correct behaviors rather than attack core identity allow a child to change without needing to alter their basic definition of themselves.

Community values and definitions also have a strong impact on children. They see those values as "real," permanent and having absolute authority. No child has the ability to discriminate, reasonably debate or challenge the existing structure of the society in which he has been born. The child is an information gatherer and an absorber of ideas and energies. When parental and community values are in agreement, the value system is even more formidable, seemingly enduring, and limiting to a child in search of self and alternatives. Greater restriction and less tolerance for diversity result when a community operates within a narrow range of ideas and values.

Damage to the evolving psyche of a child may involve feelings of unworthiness tied to insufficient nurturing and loving. What child does not deserve to be loved? Whether or not a child received adequate loving and nurturing becomes complicated by how the child perceived the experiences. Replaying the perception, and replaying the interpretation of the perception, energizes those memories until they feel like a core truth.

Rarely before adolescence does a child begin to challenge the status quo. But even when that critical capacity develops, some remain ignorant of how deeply internalized themes continue to play the role of an authoritative judge in one's own life. Rebellion, alone, does not break the powerful concepts where one's identity is held hostage to belief systems, values, and the consensus of the group. The child, in this community, also directly experiences the uniqueness that has to do with his own family of origin and the uniqueness of how he defines himself.

How do people become programmed with the untruth about themselves? Over time we have all internalized feelings of worthiness or unworthiness, deservedness or lack of deservedness, and entitlement or non-entitlement to receive.

Experiences and perceptions become messages, which then become internalized beliefs. These may feel like the core of the self, but are merely an overcoat of experiences, perceptions, and interpretations created by a child in the process of development. This overcoat of ideas may be held tightly around the self. However, there is no inherent truth in this created reality. Other sources of our sense of deservedness are the opinions of others, and internalized feelings about ourselves. The opinions of others or the criticism of ourselves can never make us feel fully deserving of love, however.

Methods of Transforming Negative Self-Talk

Energy, charged by will and intention, may assist in replacing negative repetition with positive repetition of ideas. These new energy grooves, fuelled with imagination and intention, carry the promise of change, new creation, and new manifestation. Imagination, dynamic intention, and dynamic affirmations practiced and repeated with regularity will help us harness and direct new energies of creation.

Redefining ourselves as creators of new conditions and circumstances and releasing ourselves from the imprisonment of our own ideas and consciousness will allow us to see ourselves as more than trapped victims of the past. True transformation involves the rooting up of powerful, negative energy grooves from the past. Yogis call these patterns in consciousness *samskaras*, the imprints of experiences and their results. If you truly wish to create a new, positive, affirming self-definition, you must eradicate the habit of negative self-talk. Part of the solution to uprooting this powerhouse of negation involves using the same principle of powerful, energized *positive* thought. Thoughts energized with positive affirmations, imagination and creativity, create a different powerhouse of new ideas and mental impressions, and these in turn can change your self-definition. During this process, positive affirmations remove the chatter of negative, self-limiting ideas and energy.

Perhaps the most destructive result of negative self-talk is that it blocks the more subtle vibration tied to Spirit, love, and harmony. The love vibration and spiritual light are less accessible the more your consciousness thrusts outward into the realm of activities. So if you lack integrated self-knowledge of the two selves, you block your deepest experience of yourself. As long as you feel that Spirit is separate from you, you will also believe that you cannot access the divine essence.

Without understanding your two selves, Spirit will seem separate and, in that separateness, you may feel unable to connect to happiness. And in order to achieve integration and inner peace within the Limited Self, the impediment of feelings of unworthiness must be addressed. As you redefine your deservedness, the energy lines of creation and the law of attraction and magnetism will follow. When you disrupt a powerful negative cycle, you free up energy for new creation and new lines of attraction resulting in positive manifestation.

Feelings of unworthiness and feelings that you do not fully deserve the love of others, yourself, or God poison the power that is yours in claiming the fullness of your life. Such negative self-assessment and repetitive self-dialogue can distort the fullness of the experience of being human and the fullness of the experience of being Spirit in human form. To deserve or not to deserve, that is the question. Whether it is nobler to resign yourself to a less deserved state or to risk the power of change embedded within yourself by the power of creation itself!

More on Negative Self-Talk

Ideas do not originate separate from a source. Ideas and thoughts, however, may feel as if they have always been with you. They may feel as if they are intrinsic to your self, yet the truth is they may be alien and foreign to the truth of your nature. They may be distortions that deny the true essence of your nature, your connection to Spirit, and your connection to others. Thoughts may feel as if they are true simply because you have practiced, over time, repeating them.

Exercise on Negative Self-Talk

1. Write down ten sentences you remember your father saying to you.
2. Then write down ten sentences you remember your mother saying to you.
3. If another caregiver was significant in your early life other than parents, do the exercise for that individual.

Go over those sentences and examine whether you repeat any of those sentences to yourself, either in crises or on a regular, on-going basis, not crisis-related. Do the words shape your dialogue with yourself? Or did that impression of yourself develop without input or the use of imagination and interpretation?

Will-charged affirmations and concentrated thought, explicit in visualization, will help you redefine the truth of your existence. Never doubt that the power of creation resides within you. From that source of energy, all universes, all forms, have sprung into the vibrational existence of matter. By the repetition of vibrational truth in sound, more of the potency of your own nature is unlocked. Using energized repetition in the form of spiritualized affirmations will unleash a power that can truly transform consciousness.

Some may link the idea of deservedness directly to how much faith one possesses. Some communities may judge the impulse to inquire, analyze, or question as a threat to faith. They may even equate questioning with alienation from the love of God. If you internalize such a value, you dismiss your own critical mind, which has the need and capacity to inquire and understand. In some circles, to ask is to question; to question is to doubt; to doubt is to be unworthy; to be unworthy is to be denied access to God or God's love. But the soul nature desires to know and perceive. You need to invite yourself and all, young and old, to your journey of positive exploration, supporting their ability to know, to perceive, and transform awareness in affirmative, exalting ways.

Interpretations become energized by circular replay

Feelings of unworthiness create pervasive and persistent attitudes about the right to receive. Feelings become themes. Themes repeat into a circular pattern of energy replay. The repetition deepens the theme. The deepened themes around worthiness attract similar or like energy by the law of attraction and magnetism.

Acts of mental repetition, not truth, circulate your thought energy around themes of entitlement. This energy then attracts the flow of like or similar energy by the law of attraction and magnetism. Mental ideas and thoughts are the images we replay. Mental thoughts replay into themes; the act of circular replay becomes your truth.

The Power to Limit or Create via Circular Energy Patterns

As your thoughts repeat ideas about yourself and your possibilities, you create circular energy patterns. These circular energy patterns create the energy grooves or *samskaras* that deepen by repetition. These repeated thought processes limit new possibilities, and thus limit more positive manifestation.

You become what you claim is your nature. If you make repetitive, negative statements about your tendencies and possibilities, you will find that your life reflects those statements of limitation. Similarly, if you repeat energized, positive statements by harnessing the power of focused will you will find your life reflecting new and different outcomes. You create new grooves of energy and new universes of possibilities.

Shame and Guilt

The emotions associated with guilt and shame may drastically affect your capacity to feel worthy of receiving. Yet guilt and shame may not reflect any truth about you. Sometimes guilt and shame may result from violating your values, your ideas and your perceptions of right and wrong in your life and behaviors. In those cases, the emotions may be an intuitive knowing that you have not honored life, light and spiritual laws. But very often, feelings of shame and guilt result from a restrictive childhood in which shame was a tool of discipline and adults constantly reinforced the negative to a child who was just beginning to learn, grow and become his or her self. In such situations, guilt results, though unjustly. The following clarifications may help you sort through any feelings of guilt and shame:

- Your feelings may be justified if they are based on an accurate assessment of your previous behaviors, deeds, or lack of understanding.

- If your feelings are based on accurate assessments, you will need to reshape your consciousness and behaviors.

- If you discover that you misperceived the situation that resulted in guilt or shame, then you will need to free yourself from your own powerful misunderstanding.

- Freeing yourself from such misapprehensions will also require that you reform and reshape those feelings with introspection, self-examination and explorations of consciousness and spirit.

Exploring your conscience and considering how it is formed will also help you understand more about the emotions of shame and guilt. By answering the questions below, you may shine valuable light on the issue of conscience:

- Does your conscience arise out of the messages of your childhood and environmental experiences? Or did it have its origin in a higher, intuitive, deeper place of knowing?

- What are your thoughts about conscience? Do you feel you have an over-developed conscience? Are you excessively hard on yourself over minor infractions that invoke deep, shame-based feelings?

- Do you find it difficult to connect with the feelings and emotions of other people?

- Do you see people as dispensable or disposable?

- When you view your business or career, do you feel the necessity for a moral code by which to conduct yourself?

- Do your behaviors and values involve moral considerations of honesty, disclosure, honest communication and right action in which you do not unfairly exploit the vulnerabilities of others?

- Is a lack of compassionate self-embrace advising you, constricting you or crippling you?

The Role of Conscience

Conscience is like a rudder that allows us to assess and course-correct the ship of our life. Not all feelings of guilt are invalid. Some may be divine gifts that allow us to go forward by showing us the need for other actions and behaviors that will help us create a different and better life. Those feelings may be telling us we need to more clearly examine our life course. Such feelings of guilt and shame can become helpful pointers toward a new direction. Conscience takes us to an entirely different place than animals, who operate only out of instinct.

When examining your feelings of guilt, ask yourself if those feelings might be inspiring you to make positive change. As you analyze your feelings, try to determine when your self-assessments are truly guiding you to a higher level and better direction and when your thoughts have no truth and value in the mirror of self-reflection.

Shame and guilt can result from an over-developed conscience, shame-based parenting, and community or religious ideas in which the individual felt belittled. Such personal histories may lead to feelings of being imperfect and inadequate to fully claim the status of being human, let alone being a child of God. If feelings of guilt and shame are not a rudder for self-correction, they intensify feelings of unworthiness and lack of deservedness.

As you gain clarity about which are valid messages indicating you need to correct your consciousness and actions, how can you stabilize new patterns of consciousness so you can stand fully in the sunlight of deservedness? Obviously you need to release unhealthy patterns, the self-assault with guilt and shame that may be constricting your life.

People vary widely in the development of conscience. An individual may have an under-developed conscience, while others may have an over-developed conscience. Obviously, an individual with an over-developed conscience will have more difficulties with feelings of guilt, inadequacy and shame. Strong feelings of shame and guilt may also reflect shame-based training as a child. As we have seen, those feelings may also reflect community values in which messages of spiritual inadequacy might also be part of the culture in which the child has been raised.

Guilt is usually not proportional to the deed, idea or thought with which it is associated. Your measure of guilt is not an accurate assessment of who you are or what your have done, or failed to do especially in regard to Divine order.

If any idea is constantly reinforced with powerful shame, you will begin to adopt that as a statement of truth. This statement, reinforced by repetition, then creates a distortion that you perceive as an accurate assessment and validation of who you are. Encouragingly, the experience of guilt can change if you redefine the paradigm.

Inherent Spiritual Truth versus the Idea of Indoctrination

Morality exists beyond the dogmas of religion; it is based instead on intuitive, spiritual knowing tied to spiritual principles of right and wrong. As Lord Krishna tells Arjuna, the embattled soul, in *The Bhagavad Gita*, "As unnecessary as a well is to a village on the banks of a river, so unnecessary are all scriptures to someone who has seen the truth." Often, a different morality accompanies religion and can reinforce ideas of right and wrong through *indoctrination* based on family, culture, and religious ideology. True conscience is an alignment with Truth from a spiritual perspective, but conscience can also, in some cases, be created from a set of reinforced learned ideas.

Note of clarification: The conscience that is based on a deep, intuitive knowing has its origin in the spiritual truth, divinely reflected. Intuitive knowing has its foundation and existence in the Eternal Self. The conscience of indoctrination develops out of the ideas and behaviors of individuals. Your Limited Self may develop its conscience structure out of indoctrination by ideas and the external messages from others and your interpretation of those.

Are We Worthy in the Eyes of God?

Are you worthy in your own eyes? If you hold firmly to the idea that your nature and essence is sinful and you are unworthy to experience the light of love and the glory of God, then you will be blind to who you truly are in your light nature. Your inherent deservedness is based on your nature, the truth and the power of who you really are. Any new exploration and honoring of that truth will take you to a greater state of self-realization.

From experience you may vow to extract the knowledge, the determination and understandings that may allow you to contribute to the good of your life and the lives of others. You can channel that knowing into another stream of energy. If you are wasting valuable time, energy and life force in negative circular energy around guilt, then you have an obligation to yourself to broaden your concepts and understanding. You have a spiritual obligation to liberate yourself from destructive chains of past guilt and shame. Therapy may be an invaluable tool in this process. And beyond those insights, you have a new responsibility to further create and claim the fields of light.

Redemption from Shame and Guilt by the Law of Grace

There is the grace of God and the truth of that grace is absolute. There is also a law of grace that relates to you, and when you decide and vow to take that negative circular energy and release it, you bestow the law of grace unto yourself and others in your life. No mistake is beyond redemption, for there is a higher power whose nature is love, there to always embrace you. You need to expand your love of self and others and thus redeem yourself in the light of new understandings and new motivations for change.

Substitute Negative with Positive/ Energized Intention

When you closely examine the repetitive pattern of your own thoughts, you may be able to see the bombardment of circular energy that occurs in your own consciousness. By substituting positive affirming statements for negative self-statements, you will help break negative circular thought patterns. Affirmations have the power to disrupt and fragment negative circular energy, thus becoming an effective remedy to eliminate negative self-talk. If you have spent years doubting yourself and affirming your unworthiness, simply stating, "I am loved," will not break the habit. In order to change, the thought, "I am loved," must be infused with energized intention, clearly stated, affirmed with repetition as an energized affirmation. This will create volitional energy power charged to create vibrational change and actual manifestation. You are a magnet and a generator of love itself. Affirm that truth!

Energized repetition, even if the mind does not accept the truth of the statement being repeated, will nevertheless create dynamic change. Your disbelief does not matter. State with conviction that which you desire to be expressed. State with conviction and will-charged energy and that which you desire shall come into being. The energized statement creates energy fields of movement with or without your belief. If you state truth with proper intention, will-based energy, and an observance of spiritual principles, there will be, with time, manifestation.

Thoughts are Not Neutral

An energy field of thought becomes increasingly invigorated by the energy and emotion that accompany that thought. Thoughts are not neutral. They have the power to be charged with the vibration of positive or negative energy. The thought, "I am not loved," becomes charged with powerful negative energy. Feeling states of sadness and disappointment become infused and entwined with the thought, "I am unloved." That energy operates by the law of magnetism and the law of attraction to seek its own vibrational level. The thought itself creates a state of lack. The thought itself, because it is moving with its own frequency of energy, moves on the current of repulsion rather than with the law of attraction in love. The thought of love, depending on the energized belief system, can become a magnet of attraction or a force of repulsion.

Manifesting through the art and technique of visualization also can lead to changes in your feeling of deservedness. Powerful, clearly-focused visualizations that involve intention, focused energy and gratitude often have the power to manifest. Manifestation may not occur continuously, however, unless you address the core issues that surround your feelings of worthiness and deservedness.

Why You are Deserving and Entitled

Your deservedness, as I have said many times before, is based on your spiritual nature, for your human origin is from the source of all creation, the same source of all power for manifestation. Hence you may go deeper into your own nature to utilize principles of manifestation according to spiritual law.

If you wait until you feel fully deserving, or until you feel more entitled to receive, you may wait forever! If you wait to feel "good enough," "spiritual enough," or "deserving enough" it may never come!

If, on the other hand, you make a claim based on your spiritual deservedness and the right of spiritual entitlement, you will unlock a new level of energy by which you can fuel and fuse your intention with dynamic spiritual energy. It is your right and destiny to access that energy and deepen your relationship with that force of creation.

You Are Timeless Essence

You are Timeless Essence
The promise of the light
The grand Traveler
In search of sun.

You are the joy of day
The flowering green of Spring
You are the rippling brook
And the embracing breathless moon
In search of sun.

You are Timeless Essence
Stirring creation
You are that spark of light
That ignites the sun
And warms the heart
Erupting glory of myriad possibilities
in search of sun.

You were conceived by divinity, created out of divinity, energized by the light of the sun and the stars, and you possess starlight within yourself and the star-path homeward. You possess the sunlight of possibilities and the capacity to capture divine emanations and channel the spark of new creation. The seed of all creation is within you searching for the sunlight of divine expression once again.

The stream of love and possibilities energized your form into existence. The stamp of divinity is on your brow. The divinity of all creation is in your heart. You have the power to ignite a thousand suns of possibilities because your right to receive is based on your profound status as a child of God. Your belief in that God does not change your connection to that light, that source of power and unconditional love.

You are divinity itself manifesting as the power of Love!

Affirmations of Deservedness

For The Gift of Realization
Beloved Heavenly Father,
Beloved Divine Mother,
Friend,
bestow upon me
the gift of realization.
I deserve this rightful gift
for You are mine
and I am Thine.

For Harmony in Deservedness
I act in
harmony with
that God-based
intuition NOW.
I am attuned to right action with clarity in decision-making. I am attuned to the vibration of love. From that attunement I deserve and I am entitled to all positive manifestation.

For Expansive Entitlement
I am entitled to the Good. I am entitled to the expansive love of God and the fruits of the earth.

For Deserving All Good
I claim my entitlement. I deserve the best of the earth. I deserve the divine love of the heavens. I deserve all that is good, the highest of the high.

For Divine Claiming
I claim my nature
in claiming the divine light of love.
I claim my nature
in claiming divine friendship.
I claim my nature
in loving.
I claim my nature
in friendship.

For Gratitude in Worthiness
I give thanks for
I am worthy of receiving
God's love,
God's grace.

JOHN LAWRENCE

By Jeffrey Pollack

CHAPTER FOUR

Abundance and Prosperity

You are invited to a journey of imagination, visualization, and inner discovery that will lead to greater abundance and prosperity. As you deepen your awareness of your spiritual essence and repeat affirmations of your positive spiritual essence and worthiness to receive, you will increase the positive flow in your life and your access to abundant supply.

KEY TOPICS ADDRESSED IN THIS CHAPTER:
- Your circumstances are not independent of your consciousness.
- Abundance and prosperity are not tied to material existence alone.
- The Limited Self proceeds from a perception of the finite and lack, and therefore generates and sustains attitudes in consciousness that are tied to limitation. The Limited Self can be a fear-generating mechanism.

- The Eternal Self has no perception of limitation or lack. Its nature is infinite and it operates from the perspective of the eternal and the infinite. It never participates in lack consciousness.

Because a change in consciousness is necessary for there to be a change in your material circumstances, this chapter will examine your thought patterns relating to abundance and prosperity. As you think, so you manifest. To increase your bountiful flow, you must change and claim a new powerhouse of ideas. A balanced series of activities will lead to this change: self-exploration, positive thinking, meditation, focused visualizations, and spiritual affirmations applied with will-based energy and intention. Imagination is the key. Imagination is the art of etching in the light. Etching in the light with imagination and visualization precedes your potent power to manifest.

Other supports to the manifestation of greater abundance are analysis, problem-solving, and practical approaches such as gathering information, locating resources and networking with others. These techniques will all be discussed in more detail.

Change can only begin with attention to where your consciousness is at this moment in time. You need to root out any tendencies toward self-demeaning attitudes and feelings of futility and hopelessness if you are to achieve another level of spiritual embrace and attract the abundance you seek. Deservedness issues must be confronted and new thoughts must be formulated into new habits.

All of your qualities related to your creativity, imagination, ability to visualize, and capacity to affirm are powerful generators of change. But imagination without action will result in stagnation. Visualization without accessing greater knowledge, greater information and pursuing greater understanding will result in ideas floating on clouds, ungrounded by the world under our feet on Earth.

Patient, systematic practice is required, not sporadic efforts with demands for instant results based on magical thinking. No matter how many meditations or affirmations you repeat, castles will not materialize for your enjoyment without your own efforts at construction. These practical techniques involve intention and will-based channeling of energy, analysis and rational thought, along with creativity.

The Road to Greater Abundance and Prosperity

Your view of prosperity must expand beyond narrow confines and limited ideas of wealth. None of us can define abundance as only material abundance if we are to live in a state of lasting happiness. Do you harbor a consciousness of abundance and reflective gratitude? Is your consciousness tied to fears of lack and ideas of limited supply? The universe is capable of presenting generous, magnanimous gifts and supplies. If you are to increase your receiving from the generosity of the universe, the flow is best perceived as coming from a higher universal source. Otherwise the source becomes named as "chance" or "luck." Ideas that reference "chance" and "luck" may keep you trapped in a limited mental construct tied to the Limited Self. To overcome limited concepts of abundance, you must bombard the Universe, or God, with the **certainty** of response from the Source itself. Anticipating a positive response will open the possibilities of your receiving and increasing your receptivity. Aligned with that Source we cannot fail! Strengthening your connection with that Source is paramount. Training your consciousness into the habit of appreciating the flow of the prosperous good is imperative.

Once more, then, I invite you to examine your thought patterns. Is your consciousness one of lack and insufficiency? Do you have fears about deprivation, limitations, or financial need? Such negative concentration and visualization will generate limited streams of energy. If you shift your consciousness to a view of abundance, prosperity, and expansiveness, you will shift the energy fields in a way that cultivates a boundless crop of positive circumstances and conditions.

There is no magic formula by which dreams can effortlessly materialize abundance and prosperity. However, such dreams can and do materialize with effort, energy, imagination and discipline. As in other areas, an earnest exploration of your habits in consciousness is needed. Your inner voyage of discovery brings an obligation to increase your awareness of outer circumstances and conditions around you. With that awareness comes the necessity of organizing, planning, assessing, and evaluating. Developing a plan of movement that allows flexibility and elasticity can positively increase how you participate in a flowing world of wealth, prosperity, and abundance.

Your imagination needs room to soar, but if it is not rooted in the realities of the earth, the result will be flighty ideas, ungrounded circumstances, wishful thinking and fanciful expectations. To offset your deceptive thinking you need to confront any false core ideas and replace them with positive affirmations grounded in truth.

False Core Idea about Abundance and Prosperity

> *"I am limited in my ability to acquire sufficient abundance and prosperity because of my own inadequacies and the limited material supply."*

Such a thought is rooted in any number of false ideas. Which of us has not invoked one of the following ideas and felt justified in doing so without realizing how sabotaging they are? They are the mental and verbal incantations of lack, enveloped in deservedness issues. These should bring you face-to-face with your unconscious thinking:

- My supply and resources are limited.
- I'm unable to achieve my financial goals.
- I'm unable to financially support myself.

- I can't do what I want to do and earn enough money to survive.
- Financial success and creative fulfillment do not go together.
- I have missed my opportunities to be successful. It's too late now.
- I am able to earn only "$$$." (Note how mentally placing a dollar amount around what you earn can become an affirmation in itself in which we are petitioning the universe to limit our supply to that level of money.)
- No matter how hard I work, I can't get ahead financially.
- If I just had more schooling or training, I'd be successful.
- I have bad luck. I never get a real chance to succeed.
- Things never go my way; the world is unfair.
- I will never have enough money to live the life I want.
- I will never get what I truly need and desire.
- Other people always seem to do better than I do.
- It's selfish to expect to prosper.
- To be spiritual is to be in a state of lack. (This thinking may correlate to the idea that God loves the poor more than the rich.)

Why is the core idea false?

The source of abundant supply is limitless and we can always access more of this unlimited supply.

Many people perceive supply as limited because the conditions and socio-economic structure of nations on earth are definitely limiting. But restrictive consciousness is perhaps the most limiting of all conditions that reduce your access in the material realm. You need to invite yourself to expand your vision of possibilities. The physical-material realm does not exist independently from that source of Spirit tied to its creation.

To conceive of prosperity as tied to the possession of a specific object, or class of objects, or a specific financial circumstance, limits the possibility of true abundance. You are surrounded by the abundance of oceanic waters. Financial prosperity is only one stream moving in a limitless universe. Small-minded attitudes regarding Self and supply will create inlets of trapped and confined waters. Your "I-ness" can catch the flow, which supplies all life and all universes. History offers plentiful examples of saints and even ordinary people manifesting great material and spiritual riches without tangible earthly cause or source. Jesus produced enough loaves and fishes to feed a multitude from seemingly scant provisions because he tapped into the Divine Source that constantly nurtures and continues to be accessible to anyone who attunes their consciousness to it.

Whatever your circumstances, you can increase your supply and your contentment and gratitude for your supply. Your consciousness is a fertile ground ever in need of the plowing and re-plowing with new ideas and habits.

Perhaps it is news to you that abundance and prosperity are not limited to the financial side of life. Your consciousness, ideas, and expectations play an important, if often unobserved, role in the physical circumstances of your life. You have the power to learn how to cultivate an attitude of abundance that allows us to reap the bounty of the earth and the plenty of the heavens.

The idea that material abundance ties primarily, or only, to the operation of the laws of the material world is faulty. The physical-material realm came into being, created from divine idea, distilled into light form. That energized light form enters and solidifies in the physical world. The physical laws of the universe did not create themselves or originate independently from the movement and flow of Spirit. The flow of Spirit forms and creates through the power of imagination. You, also, have the power to create through imagination. Great inventions originate as seed ideas. How exciting to contemplate the power of imagination to form ideas and images that dance in the light and then express themselves in more solid, concrete form in the physical world.

Paramahansa Yogananda makes the point that, "Imagination is not unreal; it is the borderland of what is yet to be real. Everything you imagine can be created by a will that is guided by wisdom." In the Summer 2010 issue of the *Self-Realization* magazine (available from www.yogananda-srf.org), he describes how to materialize cherished dreams and goals.

> *"Imagination is a portal through which you can transcend the imposed limitations of this world. All creative persons use this power. With wisdom and will, whatever you can imagine, and continue to imagine can become real. I tell you that things which do not exist now in this world will be created for you. Imagination can be materialized. When you develop spiritually, you can materialize your thoughts. When you sit still and let your imagination go as far as you can into the realm of your cherished dreams and goals, and if you can hold your mind to one-pointed concentration on the image of what you want to achieve, it will be shown to you in a true-to-life vision. And if you apply strong will power to realizing that vision, ultimately it will manifest—healings can be effected, successes attained, disasters in your environment lessened or avoided, seemingly impossible needs or worthy wishes fulfilled. Your mind united with your soul is such a powerful dynamo of spiritual existence! By increasing the energy*

of your concentration and calmness, you can consciously realize your connection with the unlimited realm…" (p.7)

You are a creator and a birthmother of creation. Your consciousness infuses seed ideas. These ideas grow through energized intention and the movement of Spirit. With the flow of Spirit the soil of the earth may give birth to the original seed thought. That which exists on the earth, has its origin in the Spirit of the heavens above. All of us have a spiritual responsibility to tend well to the earth and to utilize well the resources that are given to us as caregivers and tillers of the fields. But those fields are also the fields of light. As our consciousness reaches upward, we may access the infinite by the power of thoughts, ideas, and concepts. We can draw from and create with the limitless supply of the universe. Your consciousness can plow those fields of light.

Some key ideas to be considered around prosperity and abundance

- The Source of supply is limitless and infinite.
- Materialization of the supply is initiated through:

    a) **Seed Thoughts:** Seed thoughts emerge from Spirit. Conscious thought precedes physical manifestation of lack or the appearance of abundance. Energized seed thoughts of lack produce lack. Energized seed thoughts of abundance produce abundance. Manifestation follows the flow of consciousness.

    b) **Imagination and Visualization:** Both require dynamic, aligned, will-directed life force.

    c) **Dynamic Intention:** Your intention should be focused, energized concentration aligned with Spirit. Dynamic intention projects energy that manifests as dynamic willpower. Dynamic intention may be visualized. Dynamic intention may be affirmed.

d) **Affirmations:** These become intonations of truth containing the energized source of creation.

e) **Analysis and action:** These lay the foundation for new seed thoughts. Spirit needs actions before its flow can materialize.

The Law of Supply

- The supply of abundance in your life is not separate from your thoughts; feelings of deservedness and entitlement affect your prosperity.

- The Law of Supply operates through the Law of Magnetism and the Law of Attraction. Your consciousness and mental projections move along energy lines. Those energy lines seek similar vibratory energy. When these energy lines connect or merge with similar energies, they amplify. Amplified energy allows for a greater flow.

- The Law of Supply operates upon the base of previous actions, activities, and consciousness. Energy has been directed and sent forth from that which has already occurred. That energy is moving in a pattern and cycle of intentional completion.

- Previous misuse of the law of supply may be rebalanced by renewed effort and energy with positive intention. Living life with centeredness, equity, fairness and respect for others and the universal flow will generate an energy field by which the future manifestation of the good is being prepared.

Limitation and the Limited Self

The Limited Self perceives prosperity and abundance in a limited, finite fashion. Its vision is earthbound and its tools of measurement are tied to the scales and measuring stick of financial prosperity on earth. That perception constricts positive flow. Don't underestimate the magnetic power that conscious habits, visualizations, and affirmations may play. Attend to your consciousness in the Now. Your circumstances will always follow the movement of your consciousness. If you will change your circumstances, you must change your consciousness. Manifest prosperity by a prosperity consciousness filled with gratitude. Appreciation for the existing supply increases the supply, allowing us to tap into the endless abundance surrounding our lives.

Is your consciousness centered in prosperity and abundance? Do you have a sense of the power that ever sustains you, manifesting abundant supply in your life? Is your consciousness around your circumstances lacking or is there a feeling and attitude of the bounty of plenty ever manifesting? The supply is limitless. The Source that created all is the power of creation itself. Yet we exist in a physical-material world with physical-material limits. To assume that any level of physical desire will be automatically materialized simply by our wanting, needing, or desiring it, is faulty. Realities and limitations do exist in the physical realm. We live in socio-economic circumstances. Not only are there limitations of the earth, but our greatest limitation is a feeling of estrangement from our higher self, the Eternal Self. Any sense of the earth's inability to supply our needs creates greater feelings of separation and aloneness. This creates both fear and a consciousness of lack.

The consciousness of the Limited Self operates in habitual, ego-based patterns of thinking. It operates from finite ideas of limitation with insufficient awareness of the possibilities of manifestation through divine laws. Most of us have such an insufficient awareness. Ideas around our entitlement to receive, right to access and materialize prosperity directly influence the material manifestation in our lives. As we believe we deserve, we shall further create and attract to us those conditions and those circumstances. We must visualize receiving and practice gratitude for the abundance that we receive. As we think, we become. And as we project, we manifest. If we increase our awareness of our spiritual essence, we will increase our feelings of deservedness. As we affirm our positive spiritual essence and our worthiness to receive by the use of affirmations, we will increase the positive flow in our life and our access to abundant supply.

Whatever our financial circumstances, it is our mental habits and attitudes, positive or negative, that bring lack or abundance. As our efforts to align the Limited Self and the Eternal Self become more successful, we finally come to access more of the universe's supply. The universal supply will begin to manifest itself by our efforts in changing our thought patterns related to our perception of ourselves. Self-perception fosters and creates greater access to abundant supply. The power of Spirit to create, to manifest, and to materialize in harmonious cooperation continues to underlie the foundation of our existence. Each of us has the power to access that indelible power of Spirit.

Analysis and action

The idea that life will take care of itself and the flow of abundance will stream simply through the act of visualization is unrealistic. This view diminishes your power as a dynamic player: you in the act of thinking, you in the act of visualizing, and you acting to generate, solve, create and manifest. Any self-help advisor or book that recommends you engage the imagination and the creative process without channeling it and directing it by the power of your will can only yield floating, formless ideas that never achieve concrete materialization.

Whatever your present circumstances, you have the power to change them. An important step in creating change is to analyze those current circumstances. Look at your situation realistically.

Analyze it clearly. Engage in concrete analysis and problem-solving. Your ability to problem-solve, as well as to analyze, is also one of God's gifts.

Only when you honestly face where you are in any given situation can you allow imagination and creativity to be a wondrous part of the solution. Do not depend on wishful thinking; such thinking is stagnant energy, lacking the will and logic to find solutions and to apply practical plans and strategy. Too many people go to imagination, wishful thinking, and hope as the primary remedy for their circumstances, while they ignore their the minds' power to concentrate and to develop solutions and strategies. Yet rational thought is the foundation of effective problem-solving. Analysis and information-gathering precede the creative process. Manifestation requires both the mental and the physical and practical realms.

When those realms are disconnected or separate from one another, you cannot yield consistent results. To imagine or visualize abundance without analyzing present circumstances and forming an action plan, you are unlikely to produce results. An action plan involves an analysis of circumstances, a goal of problem-solving, and a list of the main steps to be achieved in order to create forward movement. A solid action plan is an excellent path toward a greater flow of good in your life. Too many books emphasize the power of the mind to imagine, without sufficiently emphasizing the practical aspect of will-directed activity and corresponding action. You could visualize affluence, abundance, and prosperity every day, yet if you do not take action, or your action is scattered and unfocused, there will be little momentum toward materializing what you desire.

In your action plan, build in small goals so you can monitor and assess results. Seeing even small movements toward positive results reinforce your ability to plan.

You are a dynamic activator with the power to set creation in motion. The power to imagine and the power to act are the twofold aspects that allow true creation. To be willing to apply logic and analysis in the design of specific plans and goals allows Spirit to pave the roadway toward solutions.

When you analyze your situation, you then can activate energy that may be used to apply dynamic willpower. Dynamic willpower is energized will. Energized will draws from the life force and the limitless sea of Spirit. Cut away the expectation that, if you desire enough, the universe will make your dreams come true for you. Instead, know that you were made with the power to create and to concentrate your force. Dynamic willpower is the thrust and generator of possibilities. It is a necessary prerequisite for manifestation to occur.

Discernment is also important in creating a greater abundant flow. The rational, analytical part of the self merges with the intuitive, reflective capacity—the left brain with the right—in order to produce true discernment. Acting with discernment prevents rash decisions, wishful thinking, unrealistic expectations and the pitfalls of foolhardiness. A discerning nature proceeds confidently toward goals that are in tune with Divine truth and true self-interest. This results in abundance at the highest levels, benefiting not only yourself but others.

Introspection Exercise

- Analyze your present circumstances.
- Analyze your financial conditions at present.
- Analyze the work that you are doing.
- Analyze five strengths in your skill sets.

Then give yourself the freedom to write down whatever thoughts come to you in terms of what you want. All people have skills. What are yours? Are you good with people? Do you possess mechanical or electronic talents? Do you see yourself as having verbal skills of persuasion, or the ability to influence others? Is there a way to employ any of your skills more usefully? Is there a way you could experiment with transferring some of your skills to a different field or job in a way that would not jeopardize your present financial circumstances? Is there an area of interest or creativity that you have always wanted to explore? Do new educational fields, trade skills or abilities beckon?

- Analyze the facts and factors in your life that are holding you back from new areas of exploration.

- Two obstacles that often prevent people from trying something new are the fear of failure and the fear of success. If you can step away from that paradigm and see yourself as an adventurer, would that allow you more freedom to pursue new activities, new interests and financial horizons?

- Analyze your goals and realistic ways to achieve them.

- If you feel you have an interest in a specific subject, or the possibility of a new career, can you acquire more experience and expertise in smaller increments rather than proceeding in a way that may create enormous risks to you and those dependent on you? Simply transferring skills does not automatically result in enough experience to justify changing careers or entering into new enterprises. Because change can be destabilizing professionally, analyzing and implementing smaller steps towards a change can create a bridge over which you may be able to walk towards new opportunities in career and creativity.Pursuing new interests part-time may allow you to create enough of a foundation that, with time, you may transition into a more positive work situation.

- Analyze the areas which you wish to pursue.

It is not necessary for you to have all of the answers, but you must become more proficient in asking questions. Be willing to **assimilate, analyze, activate** and **act** on those areas of career and creative interests. Acquiring more information or knowledge is not time lost, but time gained in a new level of mastery. People often feel that if another endeavor, enterprise or career is God's will for them, that the road will be smooth and effortless. Yet the abilities to make an effort, apply will, and energize your creative vision are gifts that you have inherited from the Divine Source Itself. The development of these attributes and skills is often part of your empowerment and divine claiming.

If you desire to increase your financial flow, you have to examine and understand your habit patterns in consciousness. You also need to understand patterns and trends in the work and financial worlds. You will become empowered by understanding more of who you are *and* by increasing your understanding of economic principles.

Expansion and expansiveness come from increasing your understanding of yourself and your world. Both elements are needed because if your consciousness is restricted around deservedness issues, no matter what financial flow comes to you, you will find a way to end up feeling you are materially deficient. If you attend to your habit patterns in consciousness and improve self-understanding, but have no understanding of the times and changes in the world of work and technology, you may encounter problems. If you stay attentive to practical matters, you will not waste time, effort, and resources in dead-ends. It is important to pay attention to projected trends, upcoming changes, and advances in technology. An expansive consciousness may not be sufficient in itself to counter a lack of practical information about the physical-material world in which you live.

The good news is that the work of self-knowing leads in the end to joy in self-knowing. In that joy you will experience your own expansiveness. Perhaps you will even experience the expansiveness of the universe and touch the face of the Infinite. If you increase self-knowing, you will see the universal flow that underlies all life, all worlds, as well as the universe of your own consciousness. When you know yourself more deeply you will accept the invitation to joy and expansiveness. Abundant resources will unfold before you, like a magic carpet of possibilities. The effort that might at first feel to be a burden of self-exploration and self-discovery, will, in the end, give you wings to fly and a limitless universe with abundant opportunities to soar.

Become a Master of Your Consciousness

Even if you are not yet a master of your circumstances, you can become a master of your consciousness. Greater mastery of your consciousness will always change your circumstances. The force of all creation resides within you. No matter how foreign that concept may seem to you, going deeper into your interiorized consciousness—by meditating in stillness—will allow you to penetrate the wealth of all knowing. You will also gain access to the streams of abundance that underlie all creation. Limitless supply is available to those who increasingly become aware of their Eternal Self and strive to remain unfettered by the limited consciousness of the Limited Self.

If you perceive limitation, increasing your alignment to Spirit will increase your perception of the abundant flow of the universe. The law of supply operates through magnanimous spiritual laws. All spiritual law is founded in the vibration of love. Love is the essence of all and permeates all creation. Your opportunity and invitation is to participate more in that vibration of love and come to experience that joy unending.

Unlock Your Mind Power

It becomes difficult to affirm greater prosperity if you are in a circumstance of dwindled resources or reduced faith. If you believe that life's blocked opportunities and reversals have created a constricted life, you may find it difficult and unrealistic to focus on the positive. Also, you may feel it's natural to keep reviewing your present situation from the perspective of lack. To continuously re-energize a lack-centered consciousness will send forth negative energy from those seed thoughts. These thoughts are powerful generators of your future conditions. You, in the present, are creating the conditions that you will inhabit in the future. Ideas have power to germinate circumstances. Ideas are not neutral. Ideas are an energized force in creation.

While it is to understand how you have reached your present circumstances, to obsess or ruminate over that which has already occurred can be counterproductive. Remember: Excessive negative re-plays restrict flow and reinforce a diminished view of yourself.

> *There exists a potent force of power in the universe that operates by the law of magnetic attraction to create either greater lack or greater abundance and prosperity.*

You have the power to unlock your mind! Your gift at image projection by imagination and the thrust of dynamic will expand as you regularly review your own consciousness. You are a creator! You are a light generator! And you have the power to access the energy of the universe and the power of the sun!

Faith alone, simply believing in the emergence of new, positive circumstances, without your own energy and initiative, will yield only disappointing results. God's ability to assist you is amplified when you use your own directed, will-based energy. Employing your own talents, abilities, and resources will attract, by the law of magnetism, new opportunities and more positive circumstances. Many people believe that positive change will result from sufficient faith or sufficiently strong appeals born of desperation. Those appeals may become new affirmations of negativity. Instead, align yourself with the creative force of all! Affirm prosperity!

Even with sufficient faith, as well as effort and application, people may remain in situations of challenge. Do negative circumstances mean that some people are less favored by God? Does prosperity mean another person is more favored by God? An excellent commentary on this idea is to be found in Weber's, *The Protestant Ethic and the Spirit of Capitalism.*

The power of positive affirmations to affect change is not tied to faith or belief. The power of positive affirmations is tied to the repetition of energized spiritual truth that affirms the greater good. With divine cooperation, in ever-greater attunement, you can then access more of the divine force in dynamic materialization.

Your faith, anchored in divine truth and spiritual law, can be sufficiently powerful to generate change. Energized repetition of ideas, either negative or positive, creates a dynamic, potent force of creation in the universe. Yet you may doubt that you are a potent creator of your own conditions and circumstances. You may look to become more faithful if you believe that your power resides in faith alone, when, in fact, belief in faith alone minimizes your dynamic ideas, imagination, and creative participation with the larger force of All.

INTROSPECTION OPPORTUNITY:

APPEAR

Summon new levels of manifestation and the appearance of abundance and prosperity in your life. You can make them APPEAR.

- <u>A</u>nalyze

    a) Analyze your present conditions and circumstances.

    b) Analyze your prosperity consciousness. (Do you believe you have a right to prosper?)

    c) Analyze whether you have given yourself *permission* to prosper and access limitless supply. Do you feel that you do not have a right to succeed and prosper? What is the origin of those thoughts and feelings? Do you carry deservedness issues? Your dynamic intention must first be fueled by your permission to prosper. Permission itself gives a powerful momentum to will. Permission unleashes and directs will-based energy.

- **P**rioritize

    a) What areas need to be changed?

    b) What positive areas could be further expanded?

    c) Create a list of areas that need to be changed, indicating some system of immediate change, and then the change that has less urgency. Everything else will fall into the middle category. You might list "1" as the most urgent and "3" as the least urgent; everything else is "2." Start with level "1." Then prioritize. Do not begin the changes on the "2" list until all of number "1" is completed.

- **P**erseverance

    Perseverance involves willed activity toward a specific goal or specified direction. Without perseverance there will be minimal creation and action. The act of volition, or movement, is driven by perseverance. Creativity is ignited by the movement of action, ideas, activities. The more that an idea, steps, or an activity is refortified and energized by perseverance, the more will is focused and expanded. Also, the power of creativity is further expanded, as well as your ability to achieve mastery of goals.

- **E**nergize your dynamic intention into purpose-driven activity. Activity needs to be activated by imagination, visualization, and a statement of intention in order for you to be a true co-creator in an abundant exchange with the universe.

- **A**ction is necessary. No change can occur without a decision to take action. Otherwise, dreams remain dreams, and visualized scenes never manifest. Imagination without action limits the possibility of significant change and movement, keeping both only in the realm of possibility. From your change list, select any item that allows you to make change by taking action. Add to your list what you fear will happen if you initiate change. Fears create stagnation and paralysis of dynamic will. Fear-based actions cripple dynamic flow and creativity and thus constrict abundance. About fears: Name them! Claim them! Eliminate them!

- **R**esearch. Be willing to investigate and explore information about areas in which you are interested. If you are considering new endeavors, or new business projects, or new ways of marketing an established product, explore relevant data. Insufficient information may limit your ability to go forward. Add creativity to your exploration of relevant information and processes.

You can keep the knowledge you have and invigorate it with new information and be willing to listen to input from experts. Be willing to pay attention to new trends and ideas. You can take those ideas and allow them to become incubated with creativity and imagination before you act. "Magical thinking" will never be more powerful than your mental constructs based on concrete realities and turned into action.

> *Again, we see that the joining of consciousness, ideas, imagination and visualization with solid analysis, information, and adequate research, can produce positive results and new possibilities.*

To create new resources and access greater abundance and prosperity, use analysis, permission to prosper, dynamic intention, and dynamic visualization, as well as affirmations, combined with the habit of gratitude. With gratitude, act *as if divine manifestation has already materialized.*

Your attitudes impact your prosperity

There is a direct relationship between your attitudes and that which is attracted to you through the law of magnetism and attraction.

And so cultivating certain attitudes will help you manifest abundance.

1. The attitude of gratitude and appreciation.
2. The attitude of thankfulness.
3. A positive attitude towards the prosperity of others.

Your attitudes are the road upon which prosperity and abundance travel. Your attitudes project dynamic energy, and can attract circumstances by the law of magnetism. Your circumstances can be altered by paying close attention to the habit patterns in your thoughts.

Introspection

- Write down your attitudes and ideas around how you see prosperity and abundance in your life. Gaining clarity about how your individualized thought patterns cluster into broader attitudes will give you specific target areas to address.
- Write down what you say to yourself when good fortune and prosperity suddenly occurs.
- Write down what you say to yourself when unexpected financial reverses, or states of lack, dominate your life. This will

help you gain insight into your attitudes and thoughts. Are you a dynamic co-Creator or a passive recipient of luck or chance circumstances. If you cannot analyze how you usually perceive and inner dialogue around your circumstances, you will find it more difficult to consciously change toward a more positive flow. You will also have difficulty identifying how changes of habit, as well as techniques such as affirmations, can help create such change in your life.

The attitude of gratitude and appreciation

You are part of a bigger picture. When you begin to see yourself as a part of the stream of the good by which the divine flow moves, you will further access not only your own supply but more of an ability and willingness to supply to others. When you mistakenly see all that you have as coming from your own efforts, or your power to make others supply your wants, needs, and desires, then you may further tighten your grip into a greater fear of lack. Your efforts have been important and your participation has been vital to that which has manifested in your life. That which exists now did not originate in a vacuum. But heightening your awareness that you are part of a larger flow of limitless abundance will increase your capacity to experience the increased flow in your consciousness, your circumstances and relationships with others.

Whatever your present level of flow, still practice the habits of gratitude and appreciation. Cultivate the habit of gratitude along with practicing more the **feeling state** of appreciation. To feel more gratitude, bring to your mind, from past memories, a situation or circumstance in which you felt grateful. Try to remember the scene and the feeling state that accompanied that. Keep revolving that theme and that feeling state in your mind. As you are in greater attunement with that feeling state, try to review your present circumstances. To the best of your ability attach that same feeling state to situations and experiences in the Now. That technique will increase your ability to feel gratitude in a broader circle of circumstances. Also, even if you do not feel particularly grateful, simply repeat, "I am grateful, I am thankful, I am a receiver of the good." Repeating that affirmation will increase your ability to feel gratitude.

By cultivating attitudes of gratitude and appreciation, the universe will respond. Your positive flow of appreciation will generate, like a magnet, a divine response. Along with cultivating appreciation, also cultivate the habit of saying "thank you" to the Divine Source. Change your relationship to being a true co-creator with the divine. See yourself as being abundantly supplied and abundantly supplying.

Appreciation and gratitude will continue to increase the greater possibilities of positive materialization in your life. Visualizing, affirming, and practicing statements of ever-greater faith in possibilities are powerful tools by which the new manifests. Being proactive in changing your consciousness empowers your life.

As your consciousness cultivates, your circumstances manifest. Proceed as if you have the power and the right of access to the limitless good of the earth. Proceed as if God will move in divine response to your intention. Proceed as if you will be successful in penetrating into that vast reservoir of abundant supply. Proceed as if success will be yours, victory and prosperity will be yours. And so shall it be.

Practice the habit of thankfulness

There is a distinction between thankfulness and gratitude. Gratitude is a feeling state and thankfulness is the expression of that state in words or thought. Thankfulness opens the road of supply by expressing the feeling of gratitude. Thankfulness takes form in words sent into the universe by verbal expression or by conscious thought and mental intention. Thankfulness is an act of volition directed by will. Will-directed energy intensifies and expands by repetition.

Gratitude, by repetition, also generates a powerful magnetized energy into the universe. It is the sentiment of the heart. Both gratitude and thankfulness project into the universal flow. Practice both mentally and verbally by giving thanks for the small, daily indications of the good, the positive, and the spiritual blessings in your life.

Giving mental and verbal thanks for the blessings you receive also brings the two selves into greater alignment and opens your relationship to the spiritual source. By the act of thankfulness you will train your mind to look at that which is supplied to you as coming from a reservoir of limitless supply. Experience the power of talking to, dialoging with, and expressing thankfulness to the Creator of All. In gratitude we expand our participation with the Divine. In thankfulness we project that love and gratitude to the Eternal Source.

A POSITIVE ATTITUDE TOWARDS THE PROSPERITY OF OTHERS

The highest intention as a human and divine player is to facilitate good on behalf of others. This is because we are all one through our common spiritual source. The other is you, and you are the other. That is the secret behind many secrets. The act of well-wishing and enthusiastic support for the good in other people's lives will create a harmonious flow for yourself and for others. You will have greater access to the good and to abundance based on a true spiritual foundation.

Guard against lack-centered attitudes and jealousy towards the good fortune of others. That is an attitude of the Limited Self, contrary to the knowing of the Eternal Self. That source that is plowing the fertile field of an expansive, abundant universe for others is tilling the soil from which you will receive the great harvest.

MAKE A GOD CONTRACT – BE A CONTRIBUTOR

A principle in tithing, based on sound spiritual principles, involves returning in some form a portion of that which has been given to you. This act acknowledges the Source that is beyond yourself. In this act you recognize that what you have received has been provided by a force beyond you. Your effort can access the flow of life, but it is not the source of the flow. To access the flow is to access the source of all which is in divine participation with you.

Be a contributor by making a real commitment to return part of that which is given to you in some way. To contribute financially, or to contribute with time, effort, or mentoring, allows you to claim and empower more of your life by participating with others, while creating greater alignment between the Limited Self and the Eternal Self.

Make a contract with yourself. What are you willing to give on a weekly, monthly, or yearly basis that can create a greater flow to others? Your giving is the vibration of love that has been given to you and is redistributed by the kindness of your heart. That kindness cooperates with the universe. Your acts of kindness create an expansive flow of generosity that creates more abundance and continuing generosity.

Mentoring – Give the gift of yourself

In addition to the principle of tithing, the principle involved in mentoring offers a sacred opportunity to nurture and nourish others. Mentoring allows talents, attributes and areas of potential growth to be cultivated, encouraged, and directed. It requires proceeding with intention and will-directed action towards increasing the beneficial good to another. Through the act of mentoring, you can nurture the potential of another, helping the sacred flame of inner light expand in the light of day. Volunteering in groups, organizations, or activities that are community-based can be another way of giving back in gratitude for that which has been given to you.

Introspection

Examine closely your own attitudes around giving.

- Do you see the act of giving to another as taking or denying yourself, or depleting the possibility of your receiving adequate supply? Are you giving to another in a manner that may make them feel indebted or obligated?

- Do you give out of a sense of duty? Do you feel your heart is restrictive in resenting giving to another? If you see your security as simply tied to your own efforts and limitations, you may feel anxious about sharing. If you have been, at times, in places of great challenges, you may have fears about letting go of that which you feel is your security. While it is not wise to give unrealistically, still you have the capacity out of your resources, finances, or time and energy to find a way to contribute. You can expand your connection to the light of others. Sharing your light will cast a new glow of possibility and may even light the pathway ahead for them.

- Assess how you give. What form does it take? Are there ways you can expand as a contributor? Write down your giving strategies.

- Assess and analyze if there is a way to increase your giving without creating undo feelings of obligation. If a gift makes another feel oppressed, it loses part of its meaning. Some gifts may best be made anonymously; other times that is not the case. The most important thing is to examine your own heart and continue to work with your own attitudes. That which is given should not be seen as simply coming from you, but from the flow of life and the universe of love. Your act of generosity continues the flow of God's generosity to you. Be a dispenser of the good, knowing you are a conduit of the force of light and love.

Introspection Opportunity: Abundance and Prosperity

As noted before, your ideas impact abundance and prosperity in your life. Write down the answers to these questions:

- Early in life, did you hear positive messages spoken about your vibrant future and your abilities and capabilities to succeed? Were specific talents, aptitudes, and abilities emphasized, encouraged and praised? Do you hear that your abilities and talents would result in financial security, abundance, and continuous supply?

- What is the content of your inner dialogue around your right to prosper? Do you repeat sentences you heard your mother or father say about your potential success or failure?

- What do you say to yourself about your entitlement or deservedness to achieve prosperity?

- In your mind, is the concept of abundance tied exclusively or primarily to financial success? Do your ideas around abundance encompass other areas of your life? What are those areas?

- Assess your ability to access the flow of abundance now and in your future endeavors? How do you view your personal ability to experience or manifest prosperity on a daily basis? What are your future projections?

- Do you feel that desiring abundance and prosperity is selfish and egotistical or perhaps, greedy?

- Do you have a conflict that views prosperity and abundance as inharmonious with spiritual desires? Do you feel that "Good people are not rich people?"

Have you given yourself permission to succeed?

Your ideas can limit, restrict and constrict the flow of abundance that comes to you. Another personal tendency may be to cast fear-bound anxieties into mental projections of the future. Sometimes you worry in advance about your future although those circumstances never come. Anxiety and fear become the screen upon which the future image is cast. A more desirable feeling to cultivate is **calmness, centeredness**, and **certainty** of God's ability to provide flow for you. If you are projecting fear, anxiety, and trepidation into visualized images of the future, you constrict the flow of the good and change that which is attracted to you. That feeling state, alone, has the power to penetrate into the process of visualization, which then energizes the negative vision. If your overall imagining of your future state of affairs is charged with negativity, how is it that a few minutes a day imagining prosperity will counter that force field of energy? That is why introspection, analyzing consciousness, and the systematic practice of working with interior calmness, visualization, and affirmation are needed to counter our negative habits.

Before you practice visualizations around abundance and prosperity, first practice imagining yourself in scenes and experiences that brought you great joy in the past. See yourself in those settings, relaxed, peaceful, and calm, as well as joyous. Use your gift of memory and imagination to embellish peaceful and joy-felt states. Intensify those remembered states of consciousness by activating evermore your gifts of imagination. Relax and pay attention to your breath patterns and feel as if you are riding the waves of incoming and outgoing breath in divine centeredness. Preferably use a quality meditation technique. If you do not have an established meditation routine or technique, you may want to pursue techniques by contacting Self-Realization Fellowship. (Self-Realization Fellowship, 3880

San Rafael Avenue, Los Angeles California 90065-3219 or online at www.yogananda-srf.org)

If you practice visualizing a prosperous and abundant future, center your energy in a place of calmness. With relaxed visualization, project positive images. Let your feelings mirror the image of prosperity and abundance! Respond with gratitude and thankfulness at being a recipient of the bounty of the earth.

To project fear energy into future imagined scenes dilutes the possibility of feeling safe and secure in the Now. How many of us have known people who survived desperate financial circumstances? Some of those individuals were forever corralled in that state of fear, where the fear of lack became their only reality no matter how much abundance or prosperity would later surround them. The experience of lack and the fear of lack left them constricted without a new vision or dream, thus impairing their ability to access, appreciate, and give gratitude for positive changes in their circumstances. The terror of lack blocked their ability to experience gratitude and thankfulness for their present life.

More on Introspection – Career and Finances:

Let us take the thought, "no matter how hard I work, I probably will only be able to generate a yearly income of X." Experiment with this idea to become more aware of your inner dialogue.

- What do you feel you will earn this year? Write that amount down on a piece of paper, based on your present circumstances.

- What do you estimate you will earn annually in the next couple of years? Then ask yourself the question, "Do I ever participate in internal dialogue that says, no matter how hard I work, I probably will never be able to earn over XXX in any given year?" If you discover that you are entering into this limiting, internal dialogue, it is critical to understand that the thought has become an energized affirmation. That energized affirmation is limiting your flow and your entitlement to prosper. The thought of a capped amount is broadcast to the universe saying: "Divine Source, please limit my supply. Make it possible that I only earn X dollars a year." By repeating this idea, materialization or manifestation at a physical-material level will follow. But if new ideas of abundance are sufficiently charged with dynamic intention and will-based action, the law of attraction will magnetize prosperity.

Remember that ideas of abundance, prosperity, and greater access are blueprints of creation, just as ideas of a cap on abundance or limit to prosperity can lead to a manifestation of lack. Often, it is not circumstances or others blocking our prosperity, but ourselves. Is it possible that you may be inadvertently blocking the flow and access to that stream of prosperity? You constrict the flow when you indulge in non-affirming dialogue.

Repetition of energy in the light will, in the end, lead to manifestation. The power of negative self-affirming exists whether you are aware of it or not. Any internalized, negative dialogue over time becomes a concrete negative affirmation, counter-productive to all.

You cannot change your present conditions without changing your attitudes around your circumstances. Even then, your previous thoughts and actions have set in motion events still in the process of coming to meet you. You are not a prisoner of that reality. Your ultimate freedom comes from understanding that your thoughts, ideas, and self-dialogue can align with the higher self of greater illumination. Remember, it is the Limited Self that participates in ideas of worthiness and dreams the dreams of non-entitlement. The Limited Self punishes, judges and chastises the self around the potential rights of entitlement. The Eternal Self is radiant with the truth that you are one with that Eternal Source unable to be truly disconnected from the limitless supply of the universe. Only your mind, thoughts, and ideas filter the streaming light of possibilities and prosperity. Emanations of new forms take shape as your mind wraps itself around a new flower and fragrance of possibility.

Golden Coffers

Golden Coffers
Heaven sent
The boundless
Bounty arrives

Riding wind waves
Of creativity
Sun driven
Finding the firmament
Of Earth

Yours for the Taking
Yours for the creating!

Visualize and affirm abundance

See yourself, visualize yourself in abundant circumstances.

The repetition and restatement of any affirmation creates an energy further empowered by visualization. Mentally practice seeing yourself in abundant circumstances. As you visualize, combine the image of abundance with powerful words affirming the truth of the dynamic supply of the universe. The universe is limitless! The universe is expanding in its own possibilities of creation! The divine is a director of creation, but we are divine creators in combined co-creation with that Dynamic Source. Your feelings, at some level, of not being good enough to adequately receive abundance, prosperity, and expansive generosity from the Divine comes from a constricted view of your worth. The spark of divinity resides in your nature. Part of the creator of all is resident within, co-creating with you in a dance of light and possibility. When did you start limiting your dreaming by a lesser vision of yourself? Ignite the flame of possibility that is within you! Flame the spark of divinity that is in divine cooperation with the truest desires of your heart.

The Divine Source is igniting possibilities and realities of ever-greater prosperity and abundance. The spark of God is co-creating with you in the divine expression of greater flow, greater light, and ever-greater prosperity and abundance. Light is your nature, love is your nature, and the Divine is manifesting in the name of that Light, and in the name of that Love. Abundance and prosperity are yours! The limitless universe awaits greater connection with you! Abundance and prosperity are your due. Mine, with one-pointed focus, the riches of the earth while the stars share their diamond brilliance. Be a star catcher and a stargazer. Treasures await!

Affirmations for Abundance and Prosperity

For Success through God
I give thanks for
I am a magnet of success.
God is opening doors
of opportunity NOW.

For Harmony and Attunement to Limitless Supply
I am in harmonious balance
With the Divine and the Universe.
That Divine Source
is materializing ever-greater abundance,
prosperity and resources in my life NOW.
I attune to the Divine Source
in harmonious co-creation.
I am receiving from the limitless supply
of the Divine and the Universe NOW."

For Abundance in the Father

> *My Father and I are One.*
> *All things whatsoever the Father hath are mine.*
> JOHN 16:15

For Material Abundance Manifesting
I give thanks for the great material abundance
manifesting in my life NOW.
Prosperity is my due!
Wealth is my claim!

For Material Abundance through Creativity
Divine creativity
is expanding
in amplified form
within me NOW.
Creativity is a conduit
for my financial prosperity
manifesting NOW.

For Creation for Within
The force of all creation is resident within me.
I am grateful.
I am thankful.
I am a receiver of the good.

For Participating in the Flow of Love
I am a dispenser of the good.
I am a participant in the universal
flow of love.

For Abundance through Creativity
Abundance and prosperity
are manifesting
through my creative endeavors
of will,
imagination,
and dynamic intention.

For Thankfulness
I give thanks for the great materialization
of abundance and prosperity
manifesting in my life NOW.

www.ingramcontent.com/pod-product-compliance
Lightning Source LLC
LaVergne TN
LVHW010317070426
835507LV00026B/3424